Dictionary
of
Investment Terms

Catharyn Martz

THOMSON

Australia · Brazil · Canada · Mexico · Singapore · Spain · United Kingdom · United States

DICTIONARY OF INVESTMENT TERMS
Catharyn Martz

COPYRIGHT © 2006 by Texere, an imprint of Thomson/South-Western, a part of The Thomson Corporation. Thomson and the Star logo are trademarks used herein under license.

Composed by: Chip Butzko, Encouragement Press, LLC

Printed in the United States of America by RR Donnelley, Crawfordsville

1 2 3 4 5 08 07 06 05
This book is printed on acid-free paper.

ISBN 0-324-20352-7

Library of Congress Cataloging in Publication Number is available. See page 188 for details.

For more information about our products, contact us at:

Thomson Learning
Academic Resource Center
1-800-423-0563

Thomson Higher Education
5191 Natorp Boulevard
Mason, Ohio 45040
USA

Dedication

I would like to thank Michael Jeffers, who asked me to write this book.

I'd also like to thank the many people at Thomson who made this book a reality. To Elizabeth Lowry, many thanks for your help with my manuscript; also to Steve Momper, Cathy Coleman, Yvonne Patton-Beard, Victoria Ortiz, and Chip Butzko, I appreciate the work that you do.

Then there are my colleagues in the brokerage business over the years: Tony, Gus, Steve, Nita, Jane, Caryn, Lorn, Kent, Julie, and Al. We worked hard, learned a lot from each other and had fun in the process. It's an honor to have known and worked with you.

Finally, I couldn't have done this project without the support of my family. To Glen and Brian, thank you for convincing me that I could do this, and for encouraging me along the way.

Introduction

One of the greatest services brokers can provide to their clients is education: about their accounts, investments, and the markets in which they trade. Clients who understand their investments will feel empowered, and are likely to be happier.

First and foremost, brokers must be familiar with their clients and their financial situations to know what investments are suitable for them. Brokers have a responsibility to teach their clients, to thoroughly explain all aspects of an investment, including risks, price and market volatility, and liquidity. Similarly, investors have an obligation to learn all they can about the investment products they are purchasing with their hard earned dollars. If they don't understand something, clients must ask questions. If the broker cannot provide satisfactory answers, the client should not make the purchase. In my years of observing the interaction between brokers and clients, it was obvious that the happiest clients where those who understood their investments. They were in better position to ride the ups and downs of the market, and became long-term clients of the broker and firm.

Education and effective communication are two key factors in a healthy broker-client relationship. Hopefully this book will encourage clients to seek out more information and confer with their brokers for a better understanding of their investments and the markets in which they trade.

Numbers

$2 broker When floor brokers of an exchange become too busy to handle all of their firm's orders, they may ask for help from another floor broker, also called a competitive trader, or $2 broker. The term comes from the time when the assisting broker was paid $2 for each round lot trade. Today their commission is negotiable.

5% Rule Dealers act as principal and buy and sell securities for their own accounts, charging a markup or markdown. The National Association of Securities Dealers (NASD) has adopted a markup policy of no more than five percent as a reasonable charge for brokerage services. This 5% rule is meant to serve as a guide; it is not a firm rule, and can be exceeded if the costs involved in a transaction justify it. The policy applies to all over-the-counter transactions including stocks, bonds, government and municipal securities. It does not apply to mutual funds, variable annuities, or securities sold in public offerings.

8-K Form 8-K is a report of unscheduled significant events or corporate changes that could be of interest to shareholders or the SEC. Examples of events that would trigger the filing of Form 8-K are disclosure of material nonpublic information about the company such as earnings advisories, mergers and acquisitions, or amendment of a corporate charter or bylaws.

9 Bond Rule The 9 Bond Rule is a New York Stock Exchange requirement that all bonds in quantities of less than ten be shown on the floor of the NYSE for at least one hour to ensure a fair chance for small investors to receive the most favorable price. Clients may request that their bond orders go straight to the over-the-counter market, where most bonds trade, but in that case the broker-dealer must act as a broker, and not as principal.

10-K Form 10-K is a detailed annual report that most publicly-traded companies must file with the SEC. A 10-K contains a comprehensive overview of a company's business and financial condition, including audited financial statements. The Sarbanes-Oxley Act phases in new deadlines for filing Form 10-K, summarized under 10-Q.

10-Q Form 10-Q is a quarterly report that is required of most publicly-traded companies. It contains unaudited financial information for the previous quarter and must be filed with the SEC within a certain number of days after the company's quarter end.

Deadlines for Forms 10-K and 10-Q under the Sarbanes-Oxley Act

Filing Year	Form 10-K Deadline	Form 10-Q Deadline
2003	90 days	45 days
2004	75 days	40 days
2005	60 days	35 days

Rule 12b-1 asset-based fees allows mutual funds to charge fees for expenses not associated with the distribution of its shares. Rule 12b-1 fees may be used for expenses such as advertising; compensation of underwriters, dealers and sales personnel; printing and mailing of prospectuses and sales literature to individuals other than current shareholders. *See also* load.

30-day visible supply Each day *The Bond Buyer* publishes information on new issue and secondary market municipal bonds. Once a week *The Bond Buyer* publishes the 30-day visible supply, a list of municipal bond issues that are expected to come to the market within the next 30 days.

60-day rollover *See* IRA rollover.

270 days Securities with maturities of less than 270 days are exempt from registration with the Securities Exchange Commission. This makes them less expensive to issue. Securities that fall within this time frame include money market instruments, such as bankers' acceptances, commercial paper, and repurchase agreements (repos).

401(k) A 401(k) is a type of company-sponsored tax-deferred retirement plan. It is a salary reduction plan, in which the employee agrees to contribute a certain percentage of wages to the 401(k) plan instead of receiving it as compensation. Contributions are pre-tax dollars. The employer has the option of matching a certain percentage of the contribution. Contribution limits for 2005 are $14,000, plus an additional $4,000 for plan participants age 50 or older. Contribution limits will be increased each year until 2006. Withdrawals from 401(k) plans are not allowed unless the participant is no longer employed by the employer maintaining the plan; the participant has reached age 59 1/2; the participant has become totally disabled; the participant can show financial hardship; the withdrawal is being made by the beneficiary of the deceased participant; or the plan is being terminated and no replacement plan is available.

403(b) plan A 403(b) plan is a tax-sheltered annuity (TSA) available to employees of state and local governments, school districts, tax-exempt religious, charitable, scientific or educational organizations. TSA purchases are made with pretax salary-reduction contributions. Participants may also make elective after-tax contributions. Contribution limits for 2005 are $14,000, plus an additional $4,000 for plan participants age 50 or older. Contribution limits will be increased each year until 2006. Withdrawals from 403(b) plans are not allowed unless the participant is no longer employed by the employer maintaining the plan; the participant has reached age 59 1/2; the participant has become totally disabled; the participant can show financial hardship; or the withdrawal is being made by the beneficiary of the deceased participant.

529 plan A 529 plan is a state-administered plan that allows a donor (parent, grandparent, or friend) to make an annual nondeductible contribution to save for a child's college education. Each state sets its own residency requirements, contribution limits, and tax incentives. As long as the child withdraws funds to cover qualified higher education expenses (QHEE), withdrawals are tax free. Withdrawals in excess of QHEE are taxable and subject to a ten percent penalty. If the original beneficiary does not attend college, the custodian of the account may change the beneficiary to another qualifying family member. A 529 plan may be opened at a bank, mutual fund, or brokerage firm. Two web sites with helpful information and links to each state's 529 plans are www.collegesavings.org, and www.savingforcollege.com. Following is a comparison of 529 plans and the Coverdell education savings plan. *See also* Coverdell education savings account.

	529 Plan	**Coverdell Education Savings Account**
Purpose	Savings plan for college tuition or other qualified education expenses at accredited colleges and universities.	Savings plan for K-12 or college qualified education expenses, including tuition, books, room & board.
Eligibility	Prepayment plan—varies by state. Savings plan—varies by state.	$2,000 maximum annual contribution may be made by individual filers with AGI of less than $95,000 and joint filers with AGI of less than $190,000. The limit is reduced for individual filers with AGI of $95,000–$110,000 or joint filers with AGI of $190,000–$220,000. You may not contribute to a Coverdell ESA if your AGI is $110,000 for individual filers, or $220,00 for joint filers.
Beneficiary	Varies by state.	Beneficiary must be less than 18 years of age, unless special needs.
Maximum Contribution	Varies by state, but federal gift tax exclusion of $11,000 applies.	$2,000 per child.
Tax Deductions	Not federally tax deductible. May be state tax deductible, depending on state rules.	Not federally tax deductible.
Account Ownership	Account is in the donor's name.	Account is in the child's name.
Rollovers and Transfers	Funds may be transferred to another child.	Funds may be transferred to another family member if the recipient is under age 30.
Maximum Age Limitations	No limits.	Account must be closed within 30 days after reaching age 30, unless a special needs beneficiary.
Distributions	Nontaxable if used for qualified higher education expenses (tuition, fees, books, supplies, room & board) at any college, university, vocational school, or postsecondary school that participates in federal student aid programs.	Same as 529 plans, plus kindergarten through grade 12 expenses (tuition, fees, academic tutoring, special services for special needs beneficiaries, books, supplies, computers, Internet access, educational software, room & board, uniforms, transportation, extended day services) at any public, private, or religious school.
Nonqualified Distributions	Taxable as ordinary income, plus ten percent penalty.	Taxable as ordinary income, plus ten percent penalty.

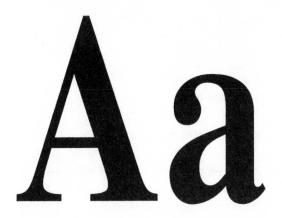

AAII *See* American Association of Individual Investors.

abandon The act of allowing an option to expire on its expiration date, rather than exercising or selling the contract.

ACATS System The Automated Customer Account Transfer Service System, used for most account transfers between brokerage firms. The NYSE and NASD require member firms to use the ACATS System, which is operated by the National Securities Clearing Corporation. A customer must open an account at the new firm, complete and sign the ACATS transfer form, and attach a copy of the most recent account statement. While the transfer is in process, a customer may not be able to trade securities and should check with both the old and the new firm before entering any orders. If the transfer proceeds smoothly, the process should take no more than six business days; margin and retirement accounts take a little longer. Some securities, such as proprietary mutual funds, may not be transferable. A client with nontransferable securities must either leave them at the old firm or sell them and transfer the cash. Partial account transfers may be done manually.

account executive *See* registered representative.

account statement The statements brokerage firms send clients who have cash or securities positions. Firms are required to send account statements on a quarterly basis; many firms mail statements more often, such as monthly, when there is activity in the account. Statements show long or short securities positions, cash credits or debits, and activity since the previous statement. It is important that customers read and understand their account statements.

accredited investor A person defined by the Securities Act of 1933 Rule 215 as eligible to make certain investments: an individual who has net worth of $1 million or who had individual income of over $200,000 or joint income with a spouse of over $300,000 in each of the two most recent years, and has a reasonable expectation of the same income in the current year. Institutions such as banks, savings and loans, broker-dealers, and entities such as retirement plans, trusts, or private business development companies have different requirements for accreditation. Some offerings and limited partnerships are open only to accredited investors. *See also* Regulation D.

accretion of bond discount An accounting process where the original issue discount of a bond is increased to reflect its cost basis as the maturity date approaches. *See also* original issue discount.

accrual accounting A method of accounting whereby income is reported when it is earned and expenses are reported when they are incurred. For an alternative method of accounting, *see also* cash basis accounting.

accrued interest Interest earned but not paid since the last interest payment date. Most bonds trade *and interest*, which means that the buyer pays the seller the purchase price of the bond plus accrued interest, which appears on both the buy and sell confirmations. Most bonds pay interest every six months on the first or fifteenth of the month; in the interim, the interest accrues. The interest payment date is called the coupon date. A kind of shorthand identifies the pattern of interest payments for bonds:

Bonds that pay interest on	. . . are called
January 1 and July 1	J & J
February 1 and August 1	F & A
March 1 and September 1	M & S
April 1 and October 1	A & O
May 1 and November 1	M & N
June 1 and December 1	J & D
January 15 and July 15	J & J 15
February 15 and August 15	F & A 15
etc.	

Example: An investor buys an M & S (March and September) bond in June. The seller will receive a full six month's interest payment in September but is only entitled to interest from March to the day before settlement date in June, after which the buyer is entitled to the interest to September. The correct accrued interest is calculated and becomes part of the dollar amount on the trade confirmation. June to September interest is added to the purchase price. Accrued interest is calculated from (and including) the last coupon payment date to (but not including) settlement date.

For corporate and municipal bonds, accrued interest is calculated using a 360-day year (30-day months). For U.S. government bonds, accrued interest is calculated using a 365-day year (actual calendar months). Accrued interest for a corporate or municipal bond using the example above would be as shown:

$$\frac{\text{Principal x Interest x Elapsed days}}{360 \text{ days}} = \text{Accrued interest}$$

Example: A municipal bond, $10,000 face value, City of Omaha, Nebraska, 5% due September 1, 2015, has a settlement date of June 18. To calculate accrued interest for the seller, we count days between the last coupon date and settlement date, using a 30-day month/360-day year:

Month	Days	
March	30	(including last coupon date of March 1)
April	30	
May	30	
June	17	(not including settlement date of June 18)
Total	**107**	

$$\frac{\$10,000 \times 5\% \times 107 \text{ days}}{360} = \$148.61 \text{ accrued interest due seller}$$

To calculate accrued interest for the buyer from settlement date until the next coupon date on September 1, we use the same procedure:

Month	Days	
June	13	(including settlement date of June 18)
July	30	
August	30	
Total	**73**	

$$\frac{\$10,000 \times 5\% \times 73 \text{ days}}{360} = \$101.39 \text{ accrued interest due buyer}$$

The buyer will receive a full six month's interest check of $250.00 on September 1. However, the buyer is not entitled to the entire amount, but has already paid the seller's accrued interest of $148.61 at the time of purchase.

For new issues of bonds, accrued interest begins on the *dated date*. For example, if an investor buys a bond in May that is going to be issued on June 1, the investor will earn interest from the dated date of June 1.

For U.S. government bonds, accrued interest is calculated using a 365-day year. The formula is as follows:

$$\frac{\text{Principal} \times \text{Interest rate} \times \dfrac{\text{Actual days}}{\text{Actual days in period}}}{2} = \text{Accrued interest}$$

Example: An investor buys a $10,000 U.S. Treasury bond, dated November 1, 1990, 8.75% due May 1, 2020, on April 9, the trade date. Regular settlement for U.S. Treasury bonds is next day, so the settlement date is April 10. To calculate the seller's accrued interest since the most recent coupon date, November 1, we use *actual days*. We need to calculate (a) accrued interest from November 1 to one business day before settlement, or April 9, and (2) the actual days of the bond's full interest period, which is November 1 through April 29.

7

Accrued Interest Actual Days		Full Interest Period Actual Days	
Month	**Days**	**Month**	**Days**
November	30 (including last coupon date of Nov. 1)	November	30
December	31	December	31
January	31	January	31
February	28	February	28
March	31	March	31
April	9 (not including settlement date of Apr. 10)	April	30
Total	**160**	**Total**	**181**

The seller's accrued interest is calculated as follows:

$$\frac{\$10,000 \ \times \ 8.75\% \ \times \ \dfrac{160}{181}}{2} \ = \ \$386.74 \ \text{accrued interest}$$

As in the municipal bond example, the buyer will receive a full six month's interest payment of $437.50 on May 1, of which she has already paid the seller $386.74 at the time of purchase. The seller's $386.74 in interest is added to the proceeds from the sale.

accumulation plan Reduced sales charges offered investors based on previous investments in the same family of funds. For example, someone who has invested a total of $50,000 may qualify for a reduced sales charge on later purchases. *See also* breakpoint.

ACH (Automated Clearing House) Network An electronic funds transfer system that processes interbank clearing of electronic payments for member financial institutions, such as direct deposit of payroll, Social Security, and tax refunds; online payment of consumer bills, such as mortgages and utility bills; business-to-business payments; e-checks; e-commerce payments; and federal, state and local tax payments.

acid-test ratio (*also called* the quick ratio) A measure of a company's liquidity, focusing on inventory. Inventory is not as liquid as other current assets. For that reason, many accountants use the acid-test ratio for a more accurate reading of how quickly a company's assets could be turned into cash. The calculation is:

$$\text{Current assets} - \text{inventory} = \text{Quick assets}$$
$$\frac{\text{Quick assets}}{\text{Current liabilities}} = \text{Acid-test ratio}$$

ACT (Automated Confirmation Transaction System) An online transaction reporting and comparison service created by the NASD. The ACT facilitates reconciliation of orders and increases the accuracy of brokerage back office operations.

active crowd *(also known as the* free crowd*)* Members of the NYSE who trade actively traded bonds or those with high volume. High volume and liquidity tend to help investors get better prices for their bonds. *See also* inactive crowd.

adjustable rate preferred stock Preferred stocks whose dividends are tied to interest rates and fluctuate as often as quarterly. *See also* preferred stock.

adjusted gross income (AGI) The amount on which most taxpayers calculate federal income tax. AGI is gross income minus allowable deductions, such as un-reimbursed business expenses and retirement plan contributions.

administrator A person appointed by a court to oversee distribution of the assets of an account holder who died intestate (without a will). Depending on the laws of the state in which the account is held, the brokerage firm should be given a copy of the court order appointing the administrator, who will then instruct the broker on disbursal of the assets in the account.

ADR (American depositary receipt) Receipts for shares of foreign corporations held on deposit at the offices of large U.S. banks in the home country of the issuer and issued to American investors instead of stock certificates. ADRs are registered with and trade on an exchange just like stocks of American companies; an example is Taiwan Semiconductor Manufacturing Company, whose ADR trades on the NYSE.

ADS (American depositary share) Individual shares of foreign stock held on deposit at the offices of large U.S. banks in the home country of the issuer; similar to ADRs and trading on U.S. exchanges, except that ADRs are receipts for a *group* of shares.

ad valorem tax *(ad valorem = a Latin term meaning "according to the value")* Taxes used, among other things, to fund many municipal general obligation (GO) bonds. A typical ad valorem tax is a property tax based on the assessed value of the property.

advance refunding Proceeds of a later issue of municipal bonds used to retire a series of bonds issued earlier at a higher interest rate. Prior to the first call date of the original bonds, the issuer sells the new bonds and the proceeds of the sale are placed in an escrow account and invested in U.S. Government securities, with the interest being used to pay the interest on the bonds to be refunded. On the first call date, the pre-refunded bonds are retired and the escrowed funds are used to pay back the investors. For example, the State of California has an issue of 5.625 percent bonds outstanding but with current interest rates being lower, the state may wish to redeem the entire issue on its first call date of May 1, 2005. The state issues a new series of bonds at four percent and puts the proceeds in an interest-bearing escrow account. On May 1, 2005, it uses that account to retire the entire 5.625 percent series.

Pre-funded Bonds	New Bonds
State of California 5.625%	State of California 4.00%
Due May 1, 2010	Due May 1, 2015
Call 5/1/05	

Prerefunded bonds are considered extremely safe because of the quality of the invested funds in the escrow account. *See also* refunding.

affiliated person *See* control stock; insider, Rule 144.

agency issue A security issued by an agency of the federal government or a federally chartered private corporation. *Examples* of such agencies are the Federal Farm Credit Bank; Federal Home Loan Banks (FHLBs); Federal Home Loan Mortgage Corporation (FHLMC); FNMA; GNMA, and Tennessee Valley Authority (TVA).

agency transaction *(also called an* agency trade*)* The purchase or sale of a security in which the broker-dealer acts as broker in buying or selling on an exchange or national market. In agency trades, the broker is paid commission. *See also* principal transaction.

agent A person who buys or sells for the account of another person. An agent takes no risk in the transaction and charges a commission for the service. A brokerage firm may act as an agent, an intermediary between buyers and sellers. *See also* principal.

aggressive investment strategy A method of portfolio management whose goal is to maximize profits; the investor therefore assumes maximum risk. An aggressive strategy may be suitable for investors who are young or who have set aside a small portion of their investment funds for that purpose.

AGI *See* adjusted gross income.

allied member A general partner of an NYSE member firm. An allied member is neither an NYSE member; an owner of five percent or more of the outstanding voting stock of the member firm; nor a principal executive director or officer of a member corporation. Allied members do not own seats on the NYSE.

all-or-none (AON) order Orders that must be executed in their entirety or not at all. AON orders may be entered as day or good-till-canceled orders. There is no limit to time, only quantity, on AON orders.

all-or-none offering A variation of a best efforts offering in which an investment banking firm, acting as agent, must sell the entire issue, or the offering will be cancelled and all investors' money is returned. SEC rules require that sale proceeds be held in an escrow account until the end of the offering. They also prohibit deceiving investors by stating that all securities in the offering have been sold if this is not the case. *See also* best effort.

alpha coefficient An estimate of projected changes in a stock price, based on factors relevant to the individual company, such as earnings, analyst expectations, or new products. For example, if the Standard & Poor's 500 index remains unchanged, a company with an alpha of 1.25 could be expected to increase 25 percent in one year. Alpha coefficients measure nonmarket risk. *See also* beta coefficient.

alternative minimum tax (AMT) An income tax designed to ensure that high-income Americans pay their share of taxes. Wealthy taxpayers with many deductions may be required to add back some taxes on certain items to raise their tax rate. AMT has two flat rates, 26 percent and 28 percent, depending on the taxpayer's filing status and income.

alternative order *(also called an* either/or order*)* An order that allows for two different courses of action; execution of one order forces cancellation of the other. *Example:* Buy 500 XYZ Corp. at $70, and Buy 500 XYZ Corp at $75 stop $80. The limit order at $70 will be executed only if the price is below $70; the stop limit order at $80 will be executed only if the price of XYZ Corp. is above $75. If one order is filled, the other will be cancelled. *See also* contingent orders.

American Association of Individual Investors (AAII) An independent not-for-profit organization whose purpose is to educate investors; a good resource for research and learning tools (web site: www.aaii.com).

American depositary receipt *See* ADR.

American option An option that may be exercised at any time between the date of purchase and the expiration date. *See also* European option.

American Stock Exchange (AMEX) A national securities exchange, located at 86 Trinity Place in New York City. The AMEX, also known as "the Curb," maintains markets in listed equities, options, exchange traded funds, bonds, derivatives, and indexes. Membership is required to buy and sell securities on the AMEX floor. The AMEX currently has 834 Regular Members, 30 Options Principal Members, and 10 Limited Trading Permit holders. Seats may be bought, sold, or leased through the Exchange's auction market or directly from seat owners. The AMEX also offers an Associate Membership, which entitles the holder to access the trading floor electronically. Where the NYSE stresses its market capital, the AMEX prefers the word "innovation"; most of the companies listing their stocks on the AMEX are smaller and newer than those listed on the NYSE. The AMEX web site, www.amex.com, is an excellent source of information.

AMT *See* alternative minimum tax.

annual report A document used by most companies to disclose corporate information to shareholders. Often elaborate, it may contain photographs and descriptions of products and subsidiaries, management discussion and analysis of the financial data, names and affiliations of members of the board of directors, and a report of the independent accountant. A companion document is Form 10-K, which has more comprehensive financial information and is filed with the SEC.

annuitant A person who invests a specified dollar amount with an insurance company in return for the company's contractual promise to make periodic payments back to that person or his or her spouse starting after a given date and continuing for a fixed period, usually the life of the investor.

annuitize To begin taking payments from an annuity. Payments may be structured in a number of ways, from monthly for a fixed amount of time through lifetime payments to one or more annuitants.

annuity A contract between an individual, the annuitant, and an insurance company. The primary difference between an annuity and a life insurance policy is that insurance policies pay when the insured person dies; an annuity is a source of income during the annuitant's lifetime.

arbitrage Generally, the practice of taking advantage of price differences between securities and markets. For example, Barney's Building Materials trades on both the NYSE and the Pacific Stock Exchange (PCX). The best price on the NYSE is bid 23.125, ask 23.25 and on the PCX, bid 23.75, ask 24. An arbitrageur would place simultaneous orders to buy at 23.25 on the NYSE and sell at 23.75 on the PCX, making a profit of 50 cents per share. *See also* index arbitrage; international arbitrage; market arbitrage; risk arbitrage; security arbitrage.

arbitrageur A person or firm engaged in arbitrage. *See the example under* arbitrage.

arbitration A method of settling a dispute between two parties in which a neutral person or panel hears arguments, evaluates evidence, imposes a judgment, and determines awards. The NASD maintains a pool of arbitrators. NASD arbitration is binding. *See also* mediation.

articles of incorporation An official document filed with the state of incorporation that outlines a corporation's purpose and the rights and liabilities of shareholders and directors; part of the corporation's charter.

asked price *See* offer.

asset Assets are what a company owns, usually consisting of current assets (cash and whatever can be converted into cash, such as accounts receivable, inventory, and prepaid expenses); fixed assets (land, buildings, equipment, and furniture); and other assets (intangibles, such as patents, licenses and trademarks, and goodwill).

asset allocation The distribution of investments in a portfolio among a variety of investment types, such as stocks, bonds, and cash equivalents. Asset allocation is an important part of diversification; it helps an investor reduce risk and increase potential return. *See also* investment pyramid.

assignee The person to whom voting rights are granted who votes stockholders' shares by proxy at corporate annual meetings if the owner of the shares is unable to attend. There is no change in ownership of the investment. *See also* proxy.

assignee of record In a transfer of ownership of a security, the new owner.

assignment The part of a stock or bond certificate, or stock or bond power, that is signed to request transfer of a security from one owner to another. All owners whose names appear on the face of the certificate must endorse the assignment.

In options, assignment is notification that the option is being exercised. For example, if Investor A has a short option position, and Investor B owns the option and elects to exercise, the Options Clearing Corporation will notify Investor A's brokerage firm that the option is being exercised and the firm will assign the exercise to Investor A's account.

assignor In a transfer of ownership of a security, the owner who makes the transfer request.

associated person Any person employed in the investment banking or securities business who is registered or exempt from registration with the NASD. This includes employees, managers, partners, officers, or directors. *See also* restricted person.

at-the-close order Orders to be executed at, or as near as possible to, the close, the end of the day's trading. Such orders must reach the trader before the end of trading, or the order is canceled.

at the market *See* market order.

at-the-money The strike price of an option that is equal to the current price of the underlying security. *Example:* A National Semiconductor March 40 call is at-the-money when the current stock price is $40 per share. *See also* in-the-money; out-of-the-money.

at-the-opening order An order to be executed at the opening, the beginning, of the day's trading. At-the-opening orders must reach the trader before the beginning of trading, or the order is canceled.

auction market A system in which buyers enter competitive bids and sellers enter competitive offers simultaneously. The listed securities on the NYSE and AMEX trade in double-auction markets. By contrast, the NASDAQ is an inter-dealer network.

authorized stock The maximum amount of stock a corporation may issue. This amount, which is approved by the state of incorporation, is stated in the company's articles of incorporation. The company is not required to issue all authorized stock; in fact, most do not. Additional authorized stock requested by the board of directors must be approved by the shareholders, and the corporate charter must be amended. *See also* issued stock; outstanding stock; treasury stock; unissued stock.

Automated Clearing House (ACH) Network *See* ACH.

Automated Confirmation Transaction (ACT) Service *See* ACT.

Automated Customer Account Transfer Service *See* ACATS.

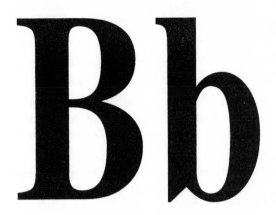

baby bond Bonds with a par value of less than $1,000, for example; $500.

back-end load Deferred sales charges; a sales charge on redemption of shares from a mutual fund. Many back-end loads are on a declining scale, depending on how many years an investor has owned the shares. *See also* load, sales charge.

| | Back-End Load |
Years Owned	Charge on Redemption
1	8%
2	7%
3	6%
4	4%
5	2.5%
6	1%
7	0%

backing away The refusal of an over-the-counter market maker to honor a firm bid or asked price for a security. The NASD's Rules of Fair Practice considers this practice unethical.

back office The departments in brokerage firms that process orders, providing the support services necessary to settle trades, keep accurate records, and comply with regulations. Though some procedures of the back-office departments may vary from firm to firm, most fall under regulations like the NASD's Uniform Practice Code. Generally, the departments include cashiering, compliance, dividends, margins, order department or wire room, purchase and sales (P&S), and reorganization.

backup withholding An Internal Revenue Service practice that encourages taxpayers to report dividend and interest income. Individuals who open accounts at institutions like banks, brokerage firms, or mutual funds must complete and sign Form W-9, Request for Taxpayer Identification Number. If the client does not complete the form or gives an incorrect number, the institution is required to withhold 28 percent of all dividends and interest as tax. The tax is nonrefundable to the client but can be claimed as tax paid.

balanced fund A mutual fund that invests in common stocks for growth, and preferred stocks and bonds for income. Most balanced funds have a preset ratio of stocks to bonds, such as 60 percent common stocks to 40 percent bonds.

balance of payments The method by which a country records its receipts from and payments to another country in a given period. If there is a surplus, more money is coming in than leaving, for example, the U.S.; if there is a deficit, more money is going out than coming in. A deficit may be created when interest rates are higher overseas, attracting investment dollars from domestic corporations and investors, and a surplus when interest rates are higher in the U.S.

balance of trade The difference between what a country exports and what it imports in a given period. A favorable balance of trade means that more goods are being exported overseas; an unfavorable balance, called a trade deficit, means that more goods are being imported than exported.

balance sheet A statement of what a company owns (assets), what it owes (liabilities), and the difference (equity) at a given point in time:

Assets = Liabilities + Shareholder equity

These three items can be broken down into subcategories:

Assets		Liabilities & Shareholder Equity	
Current assets	Cash and equivalents Accounts receivable Inventory Prepaid expenses	Current liabilities	Short-term debt Accounts payable Accrued wages
Fixed Assets	Property and equipment (less depreciation)	Long-term liabilities	6% 20-year debentures
Goodwill		Shareholder equity	Common Stock $1 par Preferred Stock $100 par Treasury stock Capital in excess of par Retained earnings
Total must match liabilities & equity		Total must match assets	

balloon maturity A time schedule for maturity of bonds in which a large number of bonds are redeemed at the end of a series. *Example:* An issuer redeems two percent of its ten-year bonds each year and redeems all the rest in the year of maturity. *See* also serial maturity; term maturity.

BAN *See* bond anticipation note.

bankers' acceptance A short-term time draft, similar to a postdated check, that has been accepted by a bank. Bankers' acceptances, which usually have a time span of one to 270 days, are often used to finance trade and can be used to pay for goods or services in a foreign country. *Example:* An American importer enters into an agreement with a company in Brazil to buy wooden toys. The American company asks its bank to send a time draft to the company in Brazil, dated six months in the future. The importer receives the toys and can sell them to generate the cash to make the payment in six months. Once the toys are shipped, the Brazilian company presents the draft for payment at its bank; after the bank subtracts a fee, the toy manufacturer receives its cash. The bank in Brazil sends the draft to the American bank for payment. The American bank "accepts" or guarantees payment on the specified date. The American bank sells the bankers' acceptance in the money market to get the cash necessary to pay the bank in Brazil. On maturity date, the American importer repays its loan at its bank and the owner of the bankers' acceptance redeems it for face value at the accepting bank.

bank grade *See* investment grade.

basis book *See* bond basis book.

basis point A measure of bond yields; one basis point is equal to .01 percent, or 1/100th of a percentage point. For example, if the yield of a bond goes from 4.50 percent to 4.25 percent. the yield has dropped 25 basis points, or .25 percent.

bear An investor who has a pessimistic outlook on a security or market, believing its trend is downward. A bearish investor might sell stock, buy put options, or sell call options.

bearer bond Unregistered, negotiable certificates with coupons representing semiannual interest payments attached. Principal and interest are payable to the holder of the bond. These may no longer be issued; new bond issues are required to be registered. *See also* registered bond, book entry.

bear market A period of declining prices for either a particular security or commodity type, such as stocks or precious metals, or the entire market.

Beige Book The common name for the *Summary of Commentary on Current Economic Conditions* issued eight times a year by the Federal Reserve Bank. The report summarizes anecdotal information gathered in each Federal Reserve Bank district through interviews with economists, market experts, key business contacts, and others.

beneficial interest A single investor's undivided financial interest in an investment like a mutual fund or a unit trust that is made up of a portfolio of securities, such as stocks or bonds.

beneficial owner The entity or individual who is entitled to the benefits of ownership, even though the title may be in a different name. *For example,* in brokerage accounts, a client may want securities held in street name, so the securities are transferred to the name of the broker-dealer, but the client remains the beneficial owner. *See also* nominee.

best effort An underwriting in which the investment banking firms, acting as agents, sell as many securities as possible to investors and return the remainder to the issuer; the investment banking firms are paid only for the securities sold. Best effort underwritings are used to sell more speculative stocks of new companies. *See also* all-or-none offering.

beta coefficient (*also known as* betas) An estimate of projected changes in a stock's price relative to increases or decreases in the market in general. Stocks with a beta of one, for example, would be expected to move with the market; if the Standard and Poor's 500 Index goes up five percent, the prices of those stocks would be expected to increase by five percent. Stocks with betas greater than one are expected to move more than the market: if the S&P 500 Index increases ten percent, a stock with a beta of 1.5 would be expected to increase 15 percent; if the market falls ten percent, the stock might drop 15 percent. Stocks with betas of less than one are expected to move less than the market. If the market rises five percent, a stock with a beta of .80 might rise four percent. In general, the higher the beta coefficient, the greater the risk. *See also* alpha coefficient.

bid price The highest price at which a dealer will buy a security from a customer. A typical quote is Bid 56, Offered 56.125. *See also* offer.

	Bid	**Offer/Ask**
Quoting dealer	Buys	Sells
Customer	Sells	Buys

Big Board A popular nickname for the New York Stock Exchange.

block trade Large orders to buy or sell. The NYSE defines a block as generally 10,000 or more shares, or any quantity worth over $200,000. Block trades may be filled in smaller increments over a period of time because the auction markets cannot absorb large orders without causing significant fluctuation in the price of the security. *See also* exchange distribution; secondary distribution; specialist block trade; special offering.

blue-chip stock The common stock of a company that is well known, has a good reputation for products and services, and has a long history of growth and dividend payments in good times and bad.

The Blue List A daily list published by Standard & Poor's of nearly every municipal bond offered in the secondary market, stating the issuer, interest rate, maturity date, price or yield, par value, and offering dealer. It contains some information about new issues.

blue-sky laws State laws regulating the issuance and trading of securities within the state. Publicly traded non-exempt securities must be registered in each state in which they may be sold. It is the responsibility of the managing underwriter to file the appropriate registration materials in the states wherever a new issue will be offered. Exempt securities include those traded on the NASDAQ National Market and exchange-listed investments. Blue-sky laws vary from state to state, but all are intended to protect investors from fraud. The term is attributed to a U.S. Supreme Court justice who described fraudulent investments as "speculative schemes that have no more basis than a patch of blue sky." The NASD Series 63 exam, Uniform Securities Agent State Law Exam, covers state licensing and registration issues, as well as fraudulent and other prohibited practices. *See also* registration by coordination, registration by notification, registration by qualification, Uniform Securities Act (USA).

board of directors The group of people elected by a corporation's shareholders to manage the corporation according to its charter. The board is usually made up of the executive officers of the corporation (called inside directors), such as the CEO, executive vice president, chief financial officer, and executives from other businesses and community leaders (called outside directors). The board is responsible for appointing company management and setting their compensation; declaring the amount and timing of dividends; and making decisions based on service on the board's audit committee, nominating and corporate governance committee, and compensation committee. The board of directors may not issue additional shares of a corporation's stock; only a corporation's shareholders may authorize their issuance. The Sarbanes-Oxley Act requires that outside directors be independent; that is, a director may not accept direct or indirect compensation other than for services as director and may not be an affiliated person. As insiders of a company, directors are control persons and any company stock they own is restricted and may be sold only under the rules of SEC Rule 144.

bona fide quote A quote where a dealer is prepared to buy or sell a security at the price quoted under the conditions accompanying the quote.

bond A loan from an investor to an issuer. Issuers can be companies, local and state municipalities, or the U.S. government or its agencies. When investors buy bonds, they are thus lending money to the issuer. The issuer promises to pay interest and repay the principal on a specific date, called the maturity date. Unlike stockholders, bondholders do not have an ownership interest in the company and do not have voting rights. Bondholders are considered creditors. If the issuer must be liquidated, bondholders are paid before stockholders, which is why bonds are also called *senior securities.*

bond anticipation note (BAN) A short-term security issued by a municipality. BANs are often issued if a municipality needs cash only briefly before a larger bond issue; proceeds from the sale of the larger issue repay BAN holders. BANs are considered money market securities.

bond attorney *See* bond counsel.

bond basis book A collection of yield tables arranged by coupon rate where the user can find yield to maturity or prices of bonds. The example below shows prices and yields at various stages of maturity for a 4.5 percent bond. *See also* interpolation.

Example of a Bond Basis Book Entry at 4.5%

Yield (%)	Years and Months to Maturity					
	12-0	12-6	13-0	13-6	14-0	14-6
4.30	101.00	101.02	101.03	101.04	101.05	101.06
4.40	100.50	100.51	100.52	100.53	100.54	100.55
4.50	100.00	100.00	100.00	100.00	100.00	100.00
4.60	99.45	99.43	99.42	99.41	99.40	99.38
4.70	98.60	98.58	98.56	98.55	98.54	98.52

The Bond Buyer The only daily newspaper devoted to the municipal bond market, providing information on both new issues and the secondary market, as well as the 30-day visible supply—a listing of all municipal offerings expected to reach the market within 30 days; the placement ratio—the percentage of the previous week's new issues that have been bought from underwriters; and new issue worksheets, for use by underwriters in preparing bids on new issues. *The Bond Buyer,* which has been published since 1891, is owned by Thomson Media.

bond contract A collection of legal documents that contain the agreements between an issuer and the underwriter of and investors in a bond issue. It incorporates the bond resolution, trust indenture, and any other legal documents required for that issue.

bond counsel A lawyer who specializes in municipal securities law and gives municipal issuers legal opinions on a bond's tax exempt status, the issuer's authority to issue the bonds, and the propriety of the issue. *See also* legal opinion.

bond fund A mutual fund that has the investment objective of income. Bond funds range from the conservative, which have a portfolio of U.S. government securities, to the aggressive, which have high-income (junk bond) portfolios. Bond funds may be made up of taxable corporate bonds or tax-exempt municipal bonds.

The Bond Guide A publication issued by Standard & Poor's Corporation that carries information on over 10,000 U.S. and Canadian corporate, convertible, and foreign bonds. It has a wealth of information about corporate bond issuers, including ratings, capitalization, assets, liabilities, and debt.

bond interest coverage *See* interest coverage ratio.

bond ladder A portfolio of bonds with different maturities that are staggered to give the investor a hedge against changes in interest rates as well as the benefit of a diversity of issuers:

Bond Ladder for a $60,000 Investment

Face Value	Issuer	Coupon	Maturity
$10,000	Bank CD	3.5%	2005
$10,000	U.S. Treasury bond	3.0%	2006
$10,000	CATS	4.0%	2007
$10,000	ABC Corp. bond	4.25%	2008
$10,000	XYZ Corp. bond	4.50%	2009
$10,000	State of California	4.25%	2010
$60,000			

By diversifying with six different issuers, the owner of this bond ladder is protected against default risk or the possibility that an issuer will not be able to pay interest or principal on its bond. When the bank CD matures in 2005, the investor may buy a new bond with a maturity of 2011. If interest rates continue to rise, the new bond will earn a higher interest rate than the 3.5 percent the CD earned, protecting the investor from interest rate risk. The investor also has $10,000 available each year, in case of a change in financial situation, such as loss of employment.

bond power A form used to transfer ownership of a bond. It contains the same information as is on the back of a bond certificate. The advantage of using a bond power is safety: it can be sent to the transfer agent separately from the bond certificate, reducing the risk of theft. *See also* assignment.

bond rating *(also called* credit rating*)* A measure of a bond issuer's ability to make interest and principal payments. Ratings services like Standard & Poor's, Moody's Investors Service, Fitch Ratings, and Duff & Phelps study a number of factors about the issuer, such as profitability, existing debt, cash flow, assets, and quality of management, to determine its financial stability. The higher the likelihood the issuer will meet its payment obligations, the higher the rating. Ratings can be changed if an issuer's financial condition changes. Revenue bonds are not rated.

Ratings play an important part in the interest rate and the pricing of a bond. A bond issued with a lower rating will need to offer a higher yield to offset the potential risk. *See also* investment grade; not rated, speculative bond.

Bond Ratings

Standard & Poor's	Moody's	Explanation
Investment Grade	*Investment Grade*	
AAA	Aaa	Highest rating
AA	Aa	Very strong rating
A	A	Somewhat susceptible to changing economic conditions
BBB	Baa	Adequate finances to pay principal and interest; slightly speculative
Speculative	*Speculative*	
BB	Ba	Speculative
B	B	Issuer has missed one or more interest or principal payments
C	Caa	No interest is being paid at this time
D	D	Issuer is in default. Payment of interest or principal is in arrears

bond ratio (*also called* debt ratio) A measure of the safety of a corporation's bonds; the ratio of the percentage of debt to assets. The formula for bond ratio is:

$$\frac{\text{Long-term debt}}{\text{Total capitalization}} = \text{Bond ratio}$$

bond resolution Authorization by a municipality to issue and sell bonds. Bond resolutions are similar to trust indentures in that they outline the issuer's responsibilities toward the bondholders. The authorizing resolution and the award resolution that authorizes the sale may be passed separately. Bond resolutions state quantity and coupon, but not price.

bond swap The simultaneous sale of one bond and purchase of another. Investors use bond swaps to improve yield or quality or to change the maturity of a bond in their portfolios. Investors who use swaps to create tax losses must be very careful to stay within the wash sale rules. The IRS does not consider it a wash sale if a bond swap involves different issuers, but the rules now allow purchase of bonds with substantially different coupon rates or maturity dates. *See also* wash sale.

bond table *See* bond basis book.

book entry The record of security ownership kept at a trust company, which sends interest and principal payments directly to the owners. Many U.S. government and municipal bond issuers as well as some mutual funds, do not issue certificates.

book value An estimate of what a shareholder might expect to receive if the company were liquidated. *See for comparison* market value.

$$\frac{\text{Shareholders equity} - \text{Par value of preferred stock} - \text{Intangible assets}}{\text{Number of shares of common stock outstanding}} = \text{Book value per share}$$

breadth-of-market theory A method of measuring the strength of the market daily by comparing the number of stocks increasing in price (advances) with the number of stocks dropping in price (declines). If advances outnumber declines, the market is bullish; in bear markets, declines outnumber advances. Technical analysts plot advances and declines on a chart to see the movement of the market over time.

breakeven point The market price that a stock must reach for an option buyer or seller to avoid a loss in exercising an option. For a call, it is the strike price plus the premium paid. For a put, it is the strike price minus the premium paid. *See also* in-the-money.

breakout The point at which the price of a stock moves outside its normal range. Stocks often trade in a relatively narrow range, with the top end being the resistance and the bottom the support level. When the price breaks out of the range and seeks new resistance and support levels, it is considered a significant move. *See also* resistance; support.

breakpoint The level of investment at which a mutual fund sales charge is reduced; in effect, a volume discount. There are two methods of qualifying for reduced sales charges: the right of accumulation, using the total value of an existing account to determine the charge for later purchases; and a statement of intention, a nonbinding agreement to invest a certain amount in a fund over a 13-month period. Breakpoints are calculated on the combined value of a client's accounts at a fund: A client with $15,000 in an IRA and $10,000 in a joint account would qualify for the $25,000 breakpoint.

ABC Fund Breakpoints

Total Amount Invested	Sales Charge (Percentage of Offering Price)
Less than $25,000	5.75%
$25,000–$49,999	5.00%
$50,000–$99,999	4.50%
$100,000–$249,999	3.50%
$250,000–499,999	2.50%
$500,000–$749,000	2.00%
$750–$999,999	1.50%
$1 million or more	Zero

breakpoint sale A broker's sale of a mutual fund to a client in an amount just under the breakpoint in order to receive a higher commission. *Example:* A mutual fund has a breakpoint of $25,000, and the broker convinces the client to invest $24,000; the client pays a higher sales charge, and the broker receives a higher payout. Such sales violate NASD rules and are considered unethical.

broad tape A continuous report of news and financial information from Associated Press, Dow Jones, Reuters, and United Press International. Because the information published could affect trading, it is not allowed on the floor of the exchanges. *See also* consolidated tape.

broker An agent (individual or company) that acts as an intermediary to arrange trades for clients and charges a commission. Unlike a dealer, a broker does not make a market or buy or sell shares for its own account. *See also* dealer.

broker call rate The interest rate banks charge brokerage firms for the funds they lend to their customers with margin accounts. The term comes from the fact that broker loans are callable on 24 hours' notice.

broker fail *See* fail to deliver.

broker loan rate *See* broker call rate.

broker's broker A broker-dealer or municipal securities dealer that acts as agent on behalf of another securities firm, not for members of the retail public.

bull An investor who has an optimistic outlook on a security or market and believes its trend is upward. A bullish investor might buy stock, buy call options, or sell put options.

bull market A period of rising prices of a particular security, a commodity, such as stocks or precious metals, or the entire market.

bunching orders The practice of combining odd-lot orders from different clients into a round lot to save the customers from the odd-lot differential. For example, a trader may have three orders to buy ABC Corp. stock: 50 shares; 25 shares; 25 shares. If they are executed individually, each client would pay an odd-lot differential. If they are combined into one round lot of 100 shares, they avoid the additional charge.

business cycle The long-term fluctuation of economic expansion and contraction.

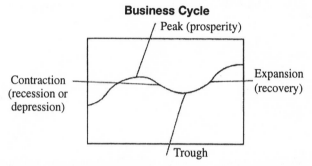

Business Cycle

Business Cycle Indicators (BCI) An index published by The Conference Board that gives figures for leading, coincident, and lagging economic indicators, as well as additional data on employment and unemployment; personal income and industrial production; interest rates and money supply; and consumer price indexes. *See also* economic indicator.

business day Any day the New York Stock Exchange (NYSE) is open for trading securities. Business days do not include weekends or holidays.

buyer's option contract An agreement to buy a security with the stipulation that the seller deliver the security to the buyer at a designated date from 6 business days to 60 calendar days after the trade date.

buy-in A purchase to rectify the problem when the broker-dealer for a seller has not sent securities in good delivery to the broker-dealer for the buyer. If after ten days the securities have not been delivered in good form, the buyer may execute a buy-in to complete the trade and charge the selling broker-dealer, regardless of the price. *See also* good delivery.

buying power The amount of fully margined securities a client could buy using the equity value of the cash and securities in the account. To calculate buying power, divide the cash balance in the account by the current Reg. T amount (50%). *Example:* If there is a cash balance of $1,000, $1,000 ÷ 50% = $2,000. If the account holds marginable securities, any excess equity can be used to purchase more securities. An account with excess equity of $2,000 has buying power of $4,000. *See also* margin.

buy stop order An order to buy at a specified price, usually above the resistance level. Buy stop orders are useful when an investor is looking for a bullish sign before committing to a stock. *Example:* A stock is currently trading at $50, its support is at $47 and resistance is at $51. If the stock breaks through resistance, which is considered bullish, the price may continue to rise. The client places an order to buy 500 shares Citigroup at $51.50 stop. When Citigroup's price reaches $51.50, that order converts to a market order and is executed at the lowest offering price available. Stop orders are accepted on all major exchanges, but not over the counter. *See also* sell stop order; stop order.

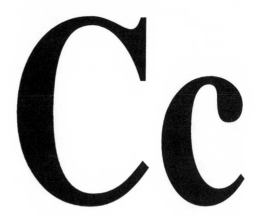

cabinet crowd *See* inactive crowd.

calendar spread (*also called* horizontal, time spread) The purchase of one option and sale of another in the same class (calls or puts on the same underlying security) but with different expiration dates, such as purchase of an ABC Mar 20 call and sale of an ABC Jan 20 call. The investor buys the option with the further expiration and sells the option with the nearer expiration. The premium of an option with a nearer expiration drops faster than the premium on the further expiration, so the investor can close the positions at a net profit. *See also* spread.

call *See* call feature.

call An option that gives the right to buy the underlying security at a predetermined price for a certain period of time. One call is a contract to buy 100 shares. *Example:* an investor buys one Microsoft Apr $27.50 call. The buyer has the right to buy 100 shares of Microsoft at $27.50 before the call's expiration in April. *See also* call buyer; call writer; option; put.

call buyer An investor who is bullish on a stock and buys a call, attempting to make a profit with as small an investment as possible. *Example:* MNO is trading at $25; 100 shares would cost $2,500. An MNO April 25 call trading at $1 costs $100. An investor who buys the stock and sells when the price goes to $30 makes a profit of $500, or 20 percent. If the investor buys the option instead, when the stock hits $30, the April 25 call would have an intrinsic value of five, or $500, and the profit would be $400, or 400 percent. The option allows the investor to realize a higher potential return on a smaller investment. If the price of MNO drops, the investor could potentially lose the entire investment with either the stock or the option if the price went to zero, but there is less risk in buying the option at $100 than the stock at $2,500.

If the price of the underlying stock had gone down or if the call buyer did not exercise the option, it would expire worthless. The loss is limited to the premium paid; the potential gain is theoretically unlimited but is limited to the increase in the price of the stock during the life of the option.

call date The date on or after which a corporation may buy back their bonds or preferred stocks. *See also* call feature.

call feature *(also called* callable, call option*)* A stated date on which a corporation may buy back its bonds or preferred stocks and pay the investors, usually at par or par plus a premium. If securities are called, dividend and interest payments cease after the call date. Corporations may, but are not required to, exercise a call provision at any time after the call date. This feature allows companies to issue new securities at lower interest rates. Call features are included in the descriptions of bonds or preferred stocks.

call loan rate The interest rate that banks charge brokerage firms for the funds they lend to customers with margin accounts. The term "call loan" comes from the fact that broker loans are callable on 24 hours' notice.

call price The price at which an issuer will pay investors to buy back a bond or preferred stock before maturity date. Call prices are usually par or par plus a premium.

call protection A feature that protects investors by forbidding bonds or preferred stocks to be called for a specified period. *Example:* A preferred stock that cannot be retired until five years from date of issue. This feature would be included in the description of the bond or preferred stock.

call provision *See* call feature.

call risk The possibility that a bond may be called before maturity. When interest rates are dropping, bonds with higher coupon rates are more likely to be called. *Example:* An investor owns a seven percent bond; new bonds pay only 4.5 percent. The seven percent is likely to be called, or retired, by the issuer. *See also* risk.

call spread The simultaneous purchase and sale of calls on the same underlying security that have different strike prices or expiration dates, or both. Bullish investors buy the call with the lower strike price, which will have a higher premium, and sell the call with the higher strike price, creating a net debit in their account. *An example* of such a debit call spread is

Buy ABC April 20 call for	4.20	(debit)
Sell ABC April 30 calls for	1.00	(credit)
	3.00	net debit

Bearish investors buy the call with the higher strike price, which will have a lower premium, and sell the call with the lower strike price. This creates a net credit in the account. An example of such a credit call spread is

Buy XYZ May 20 call for	4.20	(debit)
Sell XYZ May 15 call for	9.20	(credit)
	5.00	net credit

call writer The seller of a call; an investor who for a premium accepts the obligation to sell the underlying security at the predetermined price for a set period of time, at the discretion of the buyer. A call writer is bearish on the underlying stock. *Covered* call writing is the most conservative way to trade options, because the seller already owns the underlying stock and is willing to have it called away at a certain price. *Example:* Investor A owns 100 shares of XYZ stock bought at $20; it is now trading at $28. Investor A would be willing to sell the stock for $30. Investor A sells an XYZ May 30 call. The premium is $2.50, so the investor (the *call writer*) receives $250. Investor B, who is bullish on XYZ stock and thinks the stock will go up in price, buys the XYZ May 30 call. In May XYZ stock is trading at $30 per share. Investor B exercises the option to buy 100 XYZ at $30. Investor A's stockbroker calls to tell him that the XYZ stock has been called away at $30 per share and he will receive $3,000. Investor A is happy because he has made $1,000 profit on his XYZ stock, in addition to the $250 premium he received for the option. Investor B is happy because she can buy XYZ stock for $30 per share. Minus the premium she paid for the option, she is close to breakeven, but she believes the stock's price will go higher.

Uncovered call writing is the riskiest way to trade options. An investor who sells an XYZ May 30 call *but does not own the underlying stock* may be exposed to unlimited risk. If the option is exercised, the investor must deliver the stock, which means buying it at the current market price. There is no limit to how high the stock's price can rise.

callable *See* call feature.

callable bond A debt instrument that includes a provision for the company to repay the debt and retire the bond before the maturity date. *Example:* The General Motors 4.25% due 05/01/2021 Call 05/01/2011 @ 101.00 bond could be redeemed by GM any time after May 1, 2011 at $1,010 per $1,000 face value. *See also* call feature.

callable preferred stock A stock that the issuer may buy back (redeem) after a certain date. It allows the corporation to issue new stock with a lower dividend if interest rates drop. *Example:* ABC Corporation 6% Preferred Call 07/01/2008 @ $25 could be taken back by ABC Corporation any time after July 1, 2008 at $25 per share. *See also* call feature.

cancel former order (CFO) An instruction by a client to cancel a previous order.

can crowd *See* inactive crowd.

capital gain The profit that occurs when a capital asset, such as securities, real estate, or tangible property, is sold for more than it cost. Gains on assets held for one year or less are short-term gains; gains on assets held more than one year are long-term gains.

capitalization A company's long-term debt and net worth, which can be found in its balance sheet. Net worth is the total of stockholders' equity (capital stock, capital in excess of par and retained earnings). The formula for capitalization is:

Total capitalization = Long-term debt + Net worth

Issuing securities, redeeming bonds, or paying cash or stock dividends, which change the amount of either net worth or debt, changes the corporation's capital structure.

Market capitalization refers to the number of shares outstanding times the price per share. A company with five million shares of stock trading at $15 per share has a market capitalization of $75 million. Terms such as small-cap, mid-cap and large-cap refer to the market capitalization. *See also* bond ratio; common stock ratio; preferred stock ratio.

capital loss The loss that occurs when a capital asset, such as securities, real estate or tangible property, is sold for less than it cost. Losses on assets held for one year or less are short-term losses; losses on assets held more than one year are long-term losses.

capital market A source of funding for corporations, municipalities, and the U.S. government; the market for equity and debt securities with maturities of more than one year. Stock and bond offerings make up a large part of this market, which serves intermediate and long-term requirements, as opposed to the money market, which provides short-term funding. *See also* money market.

capital risk The possibility that investors will lose all their money under circumstances that do not involve the solvency of the issuer. Options are an excellent example of an investment with capital risk. A client may buy puts or calls and lose the cost of the premium because the options expired out-of-the-money. *See also* risk.

capital stock The total amount of common and preferred stock issued under the terms of a company's charter. *See also* shareholders' equity.

capped index option An option with a predetermined profit or cap price. The exchange sets the cap price when the option is listed. The cap interval is the number of points above, for a call, or below, for a put, the strike price. If a call or put reaches the cap price, the option is automatically exercised. *See also* index option.

capping An attempt to put selling pressure on a stock in order to move it to a lower price or keep it low, as by selling large amounts of a stock to lower the price before an option expires in order to keep clients' written calls from being exercised. This practice is prohibited by the NASD Rules of Fair Practice.

CAPS *See* convertible adjustable preferred stock.

carrying broker *See* clearing broker.

cash account (*Also called* special cash account) The basic investment account. Anyone who is eligible to own an investment account may open a cash account. In cash accounts, all purchases must be paid in full. *See also* margin account.

cash assets ratio A liquidity ratio that measures cash assets against current liabilities. The formula is:

$$\frac{\text{Cash assets}}{\text{Current liabilities}} = \text{Cash assets ratio}$$

cash basis accounting A method of accounting in which income is reported when received and expenses are reported when paid. *See also* accrual accounting.

cash dividend Distribution of a company's net profits to shareholders. Each share receives the same dividend. *Example:* A $0.15 cash dividend is declared. A shareholder who owns 100 shares will receive $15. A shareholder who owns 1,000 shares will receive $150. If the stock certificate is held by the investor, the dividend is in the form of a check; if shares are held in street name at a brokerage firm, the dividend is in the form of a credit to the shareholder's account. *See also* dividend reinvestment plan (DRIP).

cashiering department The part of a brokerage firm's back office responsible for receiving securities and sending certificates to transfer agents to be transferred, registered, and delivered to clients.

cash in advance *See* frozen account.

cash management bill (CMB) Very short-term (one to 20 day) Treasury bills that are issued to maintain the Treasury cash balance. Cash management bills are not issued on a regular basis; they are often issued in the days preceding regular tax payment dates. *See also* Treasury bill.

cash settlement *See* same-day settlement.

cash trade The request by a buyer or seller that their trades be entered for cash settlement. This means that the party on the other side of the trade agrees that the trade will be for same-day settlement. Cash settlement trades are negotiated with a premium charged to the buyer and a discount charged to the seller. Stock sold for cash settlement must be available for delivery to the other broker on trade date. *See also* same-day settlement.

catastrophe call The early, unexpected redemption of a bond if a disaster destroys the project and its revenue. *Example:* An explosion destroys a power plant that was funded through the sale of bonds. The bonds would be redeemed and the investors' money returned, usually from the insurance proceeds. Circumstances that define catastrophe calls are outlined in the bond's trust indenture. *See also* extraordinary call.

CATS (Certificates of Accrual on Treasury Securities) CATS are zero-coupon, non-callable U.S. Treasury securities sold at a deep discount. Interest accumulates over the life of the investment, which matures at face value. Because the underlying security is a Treasury instrument, they are considered safe.

CBOE *See* Chicago Board Options Exchange.

CD *See* certificate of deposit.

Certificates of Accrual on Treasury Securities *See* CATS.

Certificate of Deposit (CD) Debt securities with varying maturities, usually from 30 days to ten years, issued by banks. *Nonnegotiable* CDs are time deposits with stated maturities and interest rates. Ownership cannot be transferred from one investor to another, and the CDs can be redeemed only by the issuing bank. If they are redeemed before maturity, the issuing bank may charge a considerable penalty. *Negotiable* CDs are issued in large amounts ($1 million or more) and held on deposit at a custodian trust company. The CD is split into smaller increments and sold through brokerage firms. Most negotiable CDs have maturities of three to five years. There is an active secondary market in negotiable CDs, so that if an investor needs to redeem a CD, it can be sold at market value without a penalty. For both types of CDs, FDIC insurance guarantees deposits at member banks up to $100,000. *See also* jumbo CD.

certified financial planner (CFP) A financial planner whose expertise is attested to by the Certified Financial Planner Board of Standards. *See also* financial planner.

CFO *See* cancel former order.

CFP *See* certified financial planner.

Characteristics and Risks of Standard Options A disclosure document published by the Options Clearing Corporation that under the Securities Act of 1933 must be given to investors before or at the time they receive approval for options trading.

charter A company's articles of incorporation, combined with the certificate of incorporation. The articles of incorporation are written by the organization's owners and filed with the state, which issues a certificate of incorporation.

chartist Another name for a technical analyst who uses charts and graphs to predict prices and timing of securities trades. *See also* technical analysis.

Chicago Board Options Exchange (CBOE) The self-regulatory organization (SRO) for writing and trading standardized options.

Chicago Mercantile Exchange (CME) A futures market for interest rates, stock indexes, foreign exchange, and commodities. The CME is the largest futures exchange in the United States.

Chinese Wall A doctrine set out in the Securities Exchange Act of 1934 that requires the separation of investment banking, corporate finance, and research departments of a brokerage from the sales and trading departments. Brokerage employees in the investment banking side have access to crucial nonpublic information about the companies they work with. The SEC and the exchanges prohibit dissemination of this information to anyone who might profit from trading on it.

churning An aggressive and prohibited method of generating commissions for a broker while earning little, if any, profit for the client from excessive trading in and out of a security. It may also involve trading in quantities so large that other securities in the client's account must be liquidated to cover the purchase.

circuit breaker NYSE Rule 80B, which states that trading in all equity-related securities will be halted if the DJIA drops by ten, 20, or 30 percent. The percentages are converted to actual numerical points at the beginning of each calendar quarter. The use of circuit breakers began in 1989 in response to huge swings in the market caused by program trading. More information may be found at www.nyse.com. *See also* collar.

Circuit Breaker Trigger Points

	Before 1:00 pm*	1:00 to 1:59 pm	2:00 to 2:30 pm	After 2:30 pm
10% decline in the DJIA	1 hour halt	1 hour halt	30 minute halt	No effect
20% decline in the DJIA	2 hour halt	1 hour halt	Close for the day	Close for the day
30% decline in the DJIA	Close for the day	Close for the day	Close for the day	Close for the day

* Eastern time zone

class All options of the same type on the same underlying security; or the shares of a mutual fund that have the same characteristics. All Microsoft calls are in one class of options; all Microsoft puts are in another. Each class of mutual fund shares has its own expense structure and sales charge. Factors to consider in choosing a class of shares include how long an investor plans to own the shares; how much money will be invested; if the investor plans to take distributions; and total expenses for each class. The numerous classes of shares are described in each fund's prospectus. Some examples:

- Class A shares: initial sales charge, 5.75 percent, but lower at a $25,000 breakpoint; no deferred sales charge; 12b-1 fees of 0.25 percent; higher dividends due to reduced annual expenses.

- Class B shares: no initial sales charge; no breakpoint; deferred sales charge on shares sold starting at five percent in year one to zero percent in year seven; 12b-1 fees of one percent per year; lower dividends due to higher expenses.

- Class C shares: no initial sales charge; no breakpoint; deferred sales charge of one percent on shares sold in year one; 12b-1 fees of one percent per year; lower dividends than other classes due to higher expenses.

- Class F shares: no initial sales charge; no breakpoint; no deferred sales charge; 12b-1 fees of 0.50 percent to 0.75 percent per year; lower dividends due to higher expenses.

clearing broker A firm that clears its own trades, as well as the trades of introducing brokers. A clearing broker may hold customers' cash and securities in street name accounts. *See also* introducing broker.

clearing corporation A company that handles the delivery of securities and settlement of trades for brokerages. Clearing corporations total a firm's trades each day and reconcile each member firm's transactions against the others. They also facilitate transfer of client accounts from one broker-dealer to another. Examples are Depository Trust and Clearing Corporation (DTCC); The Clearing Corporation; and Options Clearing Corporation.

closed-end fund A type of mutual fund, issued by a closed-end management company, that issues a fixed number of shares in a stock offering and closes the offering when all the shares are distributed. Closed-end fund shares trade like stock on an exchange or over the counter at bid and ask prices, which may be different from the fund's NAV. Each share of the closed-end fund represents ownership in a portfolio of securities with a pre-determined investment objective. For example, the portfolio of a country fund, such as the India Fund or the Korea Fund, is made up of stocks of companies from that country. Investors who want to redeem closed-end fund shares sell them in the marketplace and pay a commission. *See also* mutual fund, open-end fund.

closing transaction The purchase or sale of an investment that reduces the net holdings in an account. A closing transaction to sell decreases a client's long positions. A closing transaction to buy decreases a client's short positions. *See also* opening transaction.

CMB *See* cash management bill.

CME *See* Chicago Mercantile Exchange (CME).

CMO (collateralized mortgage obligation) Mortgage-backed corporate securities issued by mortgage bankers and loan companies. CMOs, like GNMA and FNMA pass-through securities, represent large pools of home mortgages. The mortgages are separated into maturity classes, called tranches, each with an approximate maturity date based on the maturity of the mortgages in it. As homeowners make mortgage payments, the principal and interest are deposited into the pool and passed through to CMO investors. However, when interest rates drop, a large number of homeowners refinance their mortgages, which increases principal payments into the CMO pools, shortening the life of the CMO. *See also* tranche.

COBRA (Consolidated Omnibus Budget Reconciliation Act) *See* ERISA.

COD (collect on delivery) *See* delivery vs. payment.

Code of Arbitration Procedure *See* NASD Code of Arbitration Procedure.

Code of Procedure *See* NASD Code of Procedure.

coincident indicator A factor that mirrors trends in the business cycle. The Conference Board publishes the Index of Coincident Indicators monthly. The four coincident indicators are: personal income less transfer payments, manufacturing and trade sales, industrial production, and nonagricultural payroll workers. If these factors are up, the economy is expanding; if they are down, the economy is contracting.

cold calling Unsolicited telephone calls to prospective investors offering brokerage services and products. According to the NASD, broker cold calling is one of the most common problems reported by investors. Brokers are prohibited from making high-pressure, persistent phone calls outside the hours of 8 a.m. and 9 p.m. Investors who want brokers to stop calling should request to be put on the do-not-call list. If the broker continues to call, the investor should contact the firm's branch manager or compliance department immediately. *See also* NASD's "Common Investor Problems and How to Avoid Them" at www.nasd.com/Investor/Protection/best_practices.asp.

collar NYSE Rule 80A, which pertains to index arbitrage orders of component stocks of the S&P 500 Index, stating that if the DJIA drops by a predetermined amount, index arbitrage sell orders of any component stock of the S&P 500 must be marked "sell plus" and can only trade on a plus tick, and that if it rises by a predetermined amount, index arbitrage buy orders of any S&P 500 stock must be marked "buy minus" and can only trade on a minus tick. The predetermined amount of change is calculated at the beginning of each calendar quarter, using the average closing value of the DJIA for the last month of the previous quarter; the trigger is a two percent change from that amount, either up or down. The collar is removed when the DJIA reverses to one percent of the predetermined amount. Viewers of CNBC will see the note "curbs in" next to the day's change in DJIA. *For more information, see* www.nyse.com. *See also* circuit breaker.

collateralized mortgage obligation *See* CMO.

collection ratio A measure of approximately how long accounts receivable have been outstanding. If a company is efficient in collecting its receivables, its collection ratio, expressed in days, is low.

$$\frac{\text{Receivables x 360}}{\text{Net sales}} = \text{Collection ratio}$$

collect on delivery (COD) *See* delivery vs. payment (DVP).

combination Two options on the same underlying stock that differ in type (one call and one put), strike price, or expiration date. A long combination is the purchase of a call and a put on the same underlying stock with different strike prices and expiration dates; for example, the purchase of Kodak Jan 20 calls and Kodak Mar 15 puts. A short combination is the sale of a call and a put on the same underlying stock with different strike prices and expiration dates, for example, sale of Citigroup April 50 calls and Citigroup June 40 puts.

combination preferred stock An issue of preferred stock that has callable, convertible, cumulative, or participating features, or any combination of these. *See also* callable preferred stock; convertible preferred stock; cumulative preferred stock; participating preferred stock.

combined account A margin account with both long and short positions. To calculate customer equity in a combination account, subtract what is owed from what is owned:

	Market value long
plus	Credit balance
minus	Market value short
minus	Debit balance
equals	Equity

Example: An investor has a long position in stock worth $15,000, a credit balance of $5,000 cash, a short position in stock worth $5,000, and a debit balance of $6,000; the equity in the account would be $9,000:

	$15,000
plus	5,000
minus	5,000
minus	6,000
equals	**$9,000**

See also margin.

combined distribution *See* split offering.

commercial bank In the United States, a financial institution that accepts deposits backed by the FDIC. According to the Federal Reserve, as of September

30, 2001, there were 8,149 commercial banks operating in the United States. *See also* FDIC.

commercial paper Short-term, unsecured promissory notes issued by both financial and nonfinancial corporations to raise funds. Maturities are negotiable, ranging from one to 270 days. The notes are priced at a discount from face value. Interest rates are generally lower than those of commercial banks, which makes commercial paper attractive to borrowers. Most issuers of commercial paper are large corporations with good credit ratings whose notes are evaluated by the ratings services. Because the minimum investments are large, typical investors in commercial paper are money market mutual funds, retirement plans, and commercial banks. *See also* dealer paper, direct paper, prime paper.

commission A fee paid to a broker who acts on behalf of a client to buy or sell securities on an exchange or in the over-the-counter market.

commission house broker *See* floor broker.

Committee on Uniform Securities Identification Procedures *See* CUSIP number.

commodity Any bulk good that trades on an exchange or in the cash market, such as metals, grains, meats, precious metals, oil, or natural gas.

common stock An instrument representing an equity interest (ownership) in a company. Each share of stock represents a unit of equity in a company. *Example:* A company issues 100,000 shares of stock; a shareholder who buys 1,000 shares owns one percent of the company. Owners of common stock exercise ownership by electing a board of directors and voting on other matters, such as issuance of senior securities and stock splits. Common stock can be bought in an initial public offering or afterward in the secondary market. Common stockholders may have preemptive rights: if a corporation decides to raise capital by issuing more stock, it must offer the new stock to the current stockholders first, protecting their proportionate ownership in the company. When a corporation is liquidated, common stockholders have a right to the assets of the corporation, but only after creditors, bondholders, and preferred stockholders are paid. *See also* stock.

common stock ratio A measure of the degree of safety of a corporation's bonds that calculates what percentage of total capitalization is provided by common stockholders (par value, capital in excess of par, and retained earnings). The formula is:

$$\frac{\text{Common stock} + \text{Capital in excess of par} + \text{Retained earnings}}{\text{Total capitalization}} = \text{Common stock ratio}$$

competitive bid underwriting An announcement of a company's intention to issue securities, usually bonds, that asks prospective underwriters to respond with terms and price. The issuer awards the underwriting to the bidder with the best combination of highest price and lowest interest rate for the issuer. Public utilities, municipalities, and many corporations use this bid process. *See also* noncompetitive bid; underwriting agreement.

concession *See* underwriting spread.

confidence theory The theory that if investors are worried, they will invest in higher quality, high-grade bonds; if their confidence is high, they will risk investing in lower-grade bonds, which have higher yields. *Barron's Confidence Index* compares the yields of ten high-grade corporate bonds with ten intermediate-grade bonds. As more investors buy lower-grade bonds, their prices rise, lowering the yield. The spread between the yields of the higher and lower-grade bonds reflects investor confidence in the economy.

confirmation A written communication documenting a client's purchase or sale, the quantity, name of the security, price, amount of money due to or from the client, and settlement date. If the broker acts as dealer, the confirmation must disclose that fact. For every transaction, a confirmation must be sent. Confirmations are usually sent the day after trade date but may be sent up to the settlement date. *See also* when issued (WI).

Consolidated Quotation System (CQS) A service of the National Association of Securities Dealers that reports the last sale and price of listed securities in the third market, where large blocks of over-the-counter stocks are bought and sold.

Consolidated Tape A high-speed electronic system that reports the last sale price and volume of NYSE- and AMEX-listed securities, wherever the trade takes place. Network A reports trades of NYSE-listed securities; Network B reports trades of securities listed on the AMEX, BSE, CBOE, Cincinnati Stock Exchange, Chicago Stock Exchange, PCX, and PHLX. *See also* broad tape.

consolidation A term used in technical analysis to mean that a market or stock is trading in a narrow price range. In a chart, the trendline is horizontal.

Consolidation

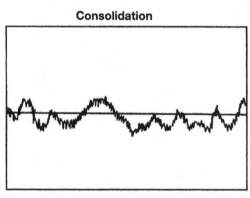

constant dollar plan A method of investing in which the investor keeps a set dollar amount invested at all times. *Example:* An investor wants to keep $50,000 invested. When the value of her portfolio drops to $45,000, she will buy $5,000 worth of securities. If the portfolio value rises to $55,000, she will sell $5,000 worth of securities. The constant dollar plan forces the investor to buy when prices are low and sell when prices are high. Its main disadvantage is that in an extended bull market the investor must keep liquidating securities instead of letting the portfolio appreciate. *See also* constant ratio plan, dollar cost averaging.

constant ratio plan A method of investing in which the investor keeps his portfolio balanced between equity and debt securities. *Example:* An investor sets a ratio of 60 percent equities to 40 percent debt. If the investor has $100,000 to invest, $60,000 must be invested at all times in equities and $40,000 in bonds. If the stocks appreciate to $70,000 while the bonds lag to $30,000, some stocks must be sold and the proceeds invested in bonds to keep the ratio constant. If the stocks appreciate by $10,000 while the bonds remain constant, $6,000 of the appreciation must be sold and the proceeds invested in bonds. *See also* constant dollar plan, dollar cost averaging.

Consumer Price Index (CPI) A monthly report published by the Bureau of Labor Statistics that tracks changes in prices paid by urban consumers of goods and services, such as food, housing, clothing, transportation, medical care, recreation, education, and communication. BLS publishes two national indexes monthly, the CPI for Urban Consumers (CPI-U) and the CPI for Urban Wage Earners and Clerical Workers (CPI-W), as well as indexes for 26 metropolitan areas. The CPI is often used as a measure of inflation, purchasing power, and income and wage adjustments.

contemporaneous trader An investor who buys or sells a security at the same time but in the opposite direction from someone who is trading on inside information. Beginning in 1988, Congress allowed contemporaneous traders to sue other investors who have violated insider trading laws. *Example:* Investor A has inside information about an upcoming announcement about XYZ Corporation and buys 1,000 shares on June 1 at $20 per share. Investor B, the contemporaneous trader, has owned XYZ Corporation stock for one year and sells 1,000 shares on June 1. On June 2 when the XYZ Corporation announcement is made, the price immediately goes to $30. Investor A sells his stock for a profit of $10,000. Investor B has the right to sue Investor A for $10,000, the amount she would have made had she not sold her stock the day before the announcement.

contingent order The simultaneous entering of two or more orders in which one order depends on the execution of the other. Contingent orders may be used in option strategies, for example, when an investor buys a stock and sells calls on the same security. *See also* alternative order.

contra broker The broker or firm on the other side of a transaction.

contraction The part of the business cycle when business activity decreases. Typical indicators of contraction are increased inventories due to decreased demand, higher consumer debt, a rising number of bankruptcies, falling stock markets, and decreasing gross national product. Depending on the length and depth of the contraction, economists may say the economy is in recession or depression. *See also* business cycle, depression; recession.

control person Someone who has a supervisory relationship with a company, such as an officer or director of the issuing company, or who owns ten percent or more of any type of the company's securities. Control persons are also called *insiders* because they have information about the company that is not public. Because of the close connection to the companies, their shares are called control stock, which is regulated under SEC Rule 144. *See also* control security, insider, Rule 144.

control security Stock owned by control persons. Control stock may be exempt from registration, but certificates of control securities are usually not so marked. *See also* Rule 144.

conversion The exchange of a convertible security for a defined amount of other securities of a corporation. *See also* convertible security; forced conversion.

conversion parity Equivalence between the value of a convertible bond or preferred stock and the value of the security into which it can be converted. *Example:* A $1,000 bond that can be converted into 40 shares of common stock is at parity when the price of the common stock is $25 ($1,000 divided by 40 = $25). The formulas for calculating parity are:

$$\frac{\text{Market price of convertible}}{\text{Conversion ratio}} = \text{Parity price of common}$$

Market price of common x Conversion ratio = Parity price of convertible

conversion price The price at which a convertible security can be exchanged for the new security. *Example:* A $1,000 bond with a conversion price of $25 means that for every $25 of par value, one share of common stock will be issued. In this case, $1,000 ÷ $25 = 40 shares of common stock.

conversion ratio The number of shares that will be received in exchange for a convertible security. *Examples:* A $1,000 bond with a conversion price of $25 has a conversion ratio of 40:1 ($1,000 ÷ $25 = 40). A $100 par preferred stock with a conversion price of $50 has a conversion ratio of 2:1 ($100 ÷ $50 = 2).

convertible adjustable preferred stock (CAPS) Convertible preferred stock on which the interest rate fluctuates with the rate of Treasury securities. Owners may exchange CAPS for common stock or cash after the next period's dividend rates are announced. The new shares have a market value equal to the par value of the CAPS.

convertible bond Corporate bond that carries the right of exchange into common stock. *Example:* An investor owns a $1,000 bond that can be converted into common stock at a conversion price of $25. This would give the owner 40 shares of common stock ($1,000 divided by $25 = 40 shares). If the price of the common stock is trading at or below $25, there would be little incentive to convert, but if it is trading above $25, the owner could convert the bond to common stock and sell the common for a profit.

convertible preferred stock Preferred stock that carries the right of exchange into common stock. *Example:* An investor owns one share of $100 par convertible preferred stock; it can be exchanged for four shares of common stock priced at $25 ($100 ÷ $25 = 4). If the price of the common stock is trading at or below $25, there would be little incentive to convert, but if it is trading above $25, the owner could convert the preferred to common and sell the common stock for a profit. The disadvantage of convertible preferred is that it generally pays a lower dividend than other classes of preferred stock. *See also* preferred stock; convertible adjustable preferred stock.

convertible security Corporate securities that can be exchanged for other securities of the same corporation; usually issued as bonds or preferred stocks. *Examples:* A $1,000 bond that can be converted into common stock at a conversion price of $25 would give the owner 40 shares of common stock ($1,000 ÷ $25 = 40 shares). The owner of one $100 share of preferred stock that is convertible into common stock would receive five shares of common at a conversion price of $20 ($100 ÷ $20 = 5).

Indentures of convertible securities state either the conversion ratio or conversion price, and the method that will be used to adjust conversion ratios or prices if there is a stock split or dividend. *See also* conversion, convertible bond, convertible preferred stock.

cooling-off period A period, usually 20 days, between the time that an issuer files a registration statement with the SEC and the public offering, during which brokers are restricted in what they may send to potential investors. They may discuss the new issue and provide preliminary prospectuses but they may not send research reports or marketing letters. *See also* preliminary prospectus, prospectus, quiet period.

corporate account A type of brokerage account. Clients who wish to open corporate accounts must provide proof in the form of a corporate resolution signed by the secretary of the corporation that the business has the legal right to own investments; the names of the officers authorized to trade in the account; and whether there is any limitation on the type of investment allowed in the account. If a margin account is requested, the corporation must provide copies of the corporate charter authorizing a margin account.

corporate charter *See* charter.

corporate resolution A document that lists the names of the officers of a corporation and contains the signature of an authorized person and the corporate seal. For the purposes of investment, the resolution names the person or persons authorized to enter orders for the corporation. This form is required to open a corporate cash account at a brokerage firm. To open a corporate margin account, the corporate resolution must state that the corporation is authorized to trade on margin.

corporation A business that is owned by its stockholders, whose ownership interest is expressed in terms of shares of stock. The ownership may change continuously with the purchase and sale of the company's stock, but the corporation continues in existence. A stockholder owner has only limited liability—the most a shareholder can lose is the amount invested in the stock.

cost basis The dollar amount paid to purchase a security or other asset. *Example:* An investor bought 100 shares of Caterpillar at $73 per share. The cost basis is $7,300 (100 x 73 = 7,300). The IRS allows adjustments for stock splits. Owners of mutual funds may use an average cost basis if the shares were acquired at various times and prices.

coterminous debt Debt issued by taxing authorities, such as cities, counties, and school districts, that overlap and collect revenues from the same taxpayers. (Coterminous means "having the same border"). In communities where there are debt restrictions, buyers of municipal bonds must be careful to accurately calculate this coterminous debt to see if other issuers have claims to the same taxes.

country risk The risk of high concentration of investments in companies located in one country. Country risk incorporates political risk, the possibility of changes in government policy, and economic risk, such as the chance of currency devaluation. Country risk occurs not only with investments in developing countries but also with investments in American companies operating overseas. *See also* risk.

coupon Bond interest. The name comes from a time when bonds had interest coupons attached that were clipped off and taken to a bank in exchange for the interest payment. The name holds even though bond interest is now paid by check or sent to brokerage firms for deposit into client accounts. If a bond has a six percent coupon, each $1,000 bond will pay the registered owner $30 every six months, $60 a year.

coupon bond *See* coupon.

coupon yield (*also called* nominal yield) The percentage of par value that an investor will earn on a bond. This percentage, which is determined at the time of issue, remains part of the description of the bond. *Example:* A $1,000 bond with a coupon yield of four percent will pay interest of $40 per year ($1,000 x 4% = $40).

covenant In trust indentures, a promise made between a bond issuer and the independent trustee who represents the bondholders. *See also* trust indenture.

Coverdell education savings account (ESA) An account to which an individual may make an annual nondeductible contribution (currently $2,000 per child per year) to save for elementary, secondary school, or college expenses so long as the beneficiary is under the age of 18. As long as withdrawals are made to cover qualified education expenses, they are tax free. Withdrawals in excess of qualified education expenses are taxable and subject to a ten percent penalty. If the original intended beneficiary does not attend college, the custodian of the account may change the beneficiary to another qualifying family member under the age of 30. Contributions not used for college must eventually go to the child, not the donor. The account must be fully withdrawn by the time the beneficiary reaches age 30. A Coverdell ESA may be opened at a bank, mutual fund, or brokerage firm. *For more information:* www.collegesavings.org, and www.savingforcollege.com. For a comparison of the Coverdell ESAand 529 plans, *see* 529 plan.

covered call writing The most conservative way to trade options because the investor already owns the underlying stock and controls the price at which it may be called away. *Example:* Investor A bought 100 shares of XYZ stock at $20; it is now trading at $28. A would be willing to sell the stock at $30, so he sells an XYZ May 30 call option for a premium of $2.50, and A receives $250. Investor B, who is bullish on XYZ stock buys the XYZ May 30 call. In May XYZ stock is trading at $30 per share. B exercises her option to buy 100 XYZ at $30. A's stockbroker calls to tell him that his XYZ stock has been called away at $30; A will receive $3,000, a $1,000 profit on his cost basis. Total profit including the option premium is $3,250.

CPI *See* Consumer Price Index.

CQS *See* Consolidated Quotation Service.

credit agreement The part of a margin agreement where the firm discloses the terms under which credit is offered. The SEC requires that customers be informed of the annual rate and method of computing interest, and circumstances in which interest rates will change. *See also* margin agreement.

credit balance (*also called* credit register (CR)) Cash that a brokerage firm is holding in a client's account.

credit call spread *See* call spread.

credit put spread *See* put spread.

credit rating *See* bond rating.

credit register *See* credit balance.

credit risk The likelihood of losing all or part of an investment due to the failure of the issuer. Credit rating services like Moody's Investors Service and Standard & Poor's Corporation analyze the financial strength of municipal and corporate bond issuers and rate their safety. Bonds backed by the U.S. government have very low credit risk. Long-term bonds generally have higher credit risk than short- to intermediate-term bonds, because the period of uncertainty is longer. *See also* bond rating; risk.

crossing orders Two market orders received by a brokerage for the same security, one a buy and the other a sell; the firm may in certain circumstances use one order to fill the other. *Example:* A member of the NYSE receives simultaneous orders to buy 1,000 shares and sell 1,000 shares of Home Depot. He must first offer the orders at a price higher than the bid by the minimum uptick, usually .125; if he wants to cross the orders at $33, he must offer the 1,000 shares at $33.125. If there is no interest, the member may cross the shares at $33.

cumulative preferred stock Securities that carry special rights regarding payment of dividends. If a corporation reduces or suspends payment of dividends, owners of common and preferred stock cannot recover unpaid dividends, but for owners of cumulative preferred stock, the dividends accumulate on the company's books. If the company at some point resumes full payment of dividends, all missed dividends must be paid to the cumulative preferred stockholders before any dividends may be paid to preferred and common stockholders. *Example:* ABC Corporation, which had been paying an annual dividend of $2 per share, suspended all dividends in 2000. It began paying dividends again in the first quarter of 2003. Cumulative preferred stockholders must receive back dividends of $6 per share ($2 for 2000, 2001, and 2002) before any other dividends can be paid. *See also* preferred stock.

cumulative voting rights One method of shareholder voting. When a board of directors is elected, each shareholder is entitled to one vote for each share owned, times the number of candidates: if there are five candidates, an owner of 100 shares would cast 500 votes. In the cumulative method, the shareholder has a choice: cast all 500 votes for one candidate or divide them among the candidates at will. This method of voting favors minority stockholders. *See also* statutory voting rights.

"curbs in" *See* circuit breaker, collar.

The Curb A popular nickname for the American Stock Exchange.

currency options A method of investing that takes advantage of changes in exchange rates between currencies. Currency options give the investor the right to buy or sell the underlying currency for a predetermined amount of U.S. dollars for a specific amount of time. Individual investors may try simply to profit from fluctuating exchange rates; multinational corporations may need to hedge against changes in exchange rates that could cost them millions of dollars. *Example:* A U.S. company selling parts to an aircraft engine manufacturer in Germany is concerned about serious losses on a multimillion dollar contract if the exchange rate between U.S. dollars and the euro changed significantly; it buys currency futures to hedge the loss. The PHLX offers standardized options on six currencies: Australian dollar, British pound, Canadian dollar, euro, Japanese yen, and Swiss franc.

current ratio *See* liquidity ratio.

current yield The annual return on an investment shown as a percentage of market value. Current yield addresses only income, not price increases. The current yield of a common stock is calculated as follows:

$$\frac{\text{Annual dividends per share}}{\text{Market value per share}} = \text{Current yield}$$

The current yield of a bond is calculated as follows:

$$\frac{\text{Annual interest}}{\text{Current market price}} = \text{Current yield}$$

The current yield of a mutual fund is calculated using the offering price:

$$\frac{\text{Annual dividend}}{\text{Current offering price}} = \text{Current yield}$$

CUSIP Committee on Uniform Securities Identification Procedures.

CUSIP number A nine-digit number that identifies issues of securities, developed by CUSIP. Each type of security issued by a company (common stock, preferred stock, bonds) has its own CUSIP number that is recognized by any brokerage firm or transfer agent. CUSIP numbers make it easier to work with securities in a computer-based environment.

custodial account *See* Uniform Transfer to Minors Act.

custodian A fiduciary of an account opened under UTMA who may buy or sell securities and manage the account until the child reaches the age of majority. At that time the child takes control of the account. *See also* fiduciary, Uniform Transfer to Minors Act.

custodian bank A bank or stock exchange member firm holding on deposit securities of mutual funds, as required by the Investment Company Act of 1940. The securities must be held in a separate account with access restricted to officers and employees of the investment company who have been appointed by the investment company's board of directors. The securities must be verified by an independent auditor at least three times a year.

customer A member of the general public who is not a broker, dealer, or NASD member.

customer protection rule SEC Rule, which requires broker-dealers to establish separate accounts in which customer credit balances are maintained; prohibits firms from using customer balances to finance their own trading; and requires firms to hold customers' fully paid and excess margin securities in an account separate from the firm's.

customer statement *See* account statement.

cycle The four expiration months through the year of each class of listed options. Cycles are January, April, July, October (JAJO); February, May, August, November (FMAN); and March, June, September, December (MJSD). If Microsoft has options expiring in January, April, July, and October, the OCC will create new options when the October options expire. Options expire on the Saturday immediately following the third Friday of the expiration month. Equity LEAPS expire in January of every year. Index LEAPS expire in January and December of every year.

cyclical industry One which is highly affected by changes in the business cycle. Most cyclical industries produce durable goods such as capital goods, steel, cement, aluminum, and heavy equipment. During recessionary periods and bear markets, cyclical stocks may have the biggest declines. Their strength is during bull markets, when they show the largest gains. During periods of inflation or high interest rates, big business postpones purchase of capital goods; and individual consumers postpone purchases of homes, automobiles, or appliances, and don't dine out as much. Cyclical stocks have the most risk but also the opportunity for a high return on investment.

dated date The date on which interest on a bond begins to accrue. *See also* accrued interest.

day order An order without a stipulated time; unfilled orders expire at the close of trading on the day they were entered. Market orders are entered as day orders. *See also* good-till-canceled (GTC) order.

day trade The purchase and sale of, or the short sale and purchase of, the same security in the same day.

day trader An investor who owns securities for a very short time, buying and selling them in the same day. Day trading is extremely risky. Even in a bull market, the odds of finding a stock that will increase enough in one day for the investor to make a net profit are small. By the time the day trader pays commissions on the buy and sell sides and accounts for the spread, any profits are likely to disappear. A pattern day trader is an investor who executes four or more day trades in five business days, provided the number of day trades is more than six percent of the total trades in the account during that period. The SEC has set new margin rules for pattern day traders, one of which sets the minimum margin equity requirement at $25,000. For non-pattern day traders, the minimum margin remains at $2,000.

DBCC *See* NASD District Business Conduct Committee.

dealer A principal who buys and sells securities for his own account. Unlike a broker, a dealer may make a market in a particular security. Instead of commission, dealers charge a markup or markdown. A brokerage firm may act as dealer if the firm makes a market in a security and buys and sells securities for its own account. Customer confirmations must state if the firm has acted as principal on dealer trades. *See also* broker.

dealer paper Commercial paper sold by the issuer through a dealer firm, rather than directly to investors. *See also* commercial paper, direct paper, prime paper.

debenture (*also called* unsecured bond) A bond backed only by the credit of the issuer. Subordinated debentures rank lower than other debentures in claims on assets of a corporation.

debit balance (*also called* debit register (DR)) The amount of cash a client owes to a brokerage firm. In margin accounts, interest is charged on debit balances, which increases the amount owed by the customer.

debit call spread *See* call spread.

debit put spread *See* put spread.

debit register *See* debit balance.

debt ratio (*also called* bond ratio) A measure of the safety of a corporation's bonds that compares percentage of debt to assets. The formula for debt ratio is:

$$\frac{\text{Long-term debt}}{\text{Total capitalization}} = \text{Debt ratio}$$

debt security Investments that represent a loan to a company, municipality, or government agency, such as bonds. *See also* equity security.

debt service The funds required to pay principal, interest, and sinking fund expenses on debt. Debt service also pertains to an issuer's method of calculating interest and principal payments over the life of a bond. In level debt service, payments to bondholders are the same amount each time, but the amounts of interest and principal change, the principal amount repaid increasing as the amount of interest falls:

Level Debt Service Payments

January 15, 2003	January 15, 2008	January 15, 2013
Interest $750	Interest $500	Interest $250
Principal 250	Principal 500	Principal 750
Total $1,000	Total $1,000	Total $1,000

With decreasing debt service, the issuer repays an equal amount of principal each time. Because this decreases total debt, which reduces the interest, the total payment is smaller each time:

Decreasing Debt Service Payments

January 15, 2003	January 15, 2008	January 15, 2013
Interest $250	Interest $200	Interest $150
Principal 750	Principal 750	Principal 750
Total $1,000	Total $950	Total $900

debt service ratio A measure of a corporation's ability to meet principal and interest payments on bonds.

$$\frac{\text{Earnings before interest and taxes (EBIT)}}{\text{Annual interest + Principal payments}} = \text{Debt service ratio}$$

debt-to-equity ratio A measure of the leverage a company has to use borrowed capital, such as proceeds from a bond offering, to increase earnings. A high debt-to-equity ratio may indicate future problems in meeting financial obligations. The formula for debt-to-equity ratio is:

$$\frac{\text{Total long-term debt}}{\text{Total shareholders' equity}} = \text{Debt-to-equity ratio}$$

declaration date The date on which the board of directors of a corporation announces a cash or stock dividend to be paid to shareholders of record. The declaration includes the amount of the dividend, the record date, and the payable date. For an explanation of the relationships between the various dates related to dividends, *see* ex-dividend date.

decreasing debt service *See* debt service.

default The failure of a bond issuer to pay interest or principal when due.

default risk The possibility that part or all of an investment will be lost due to the failure of the issuer. *See* bond ladder, bond rating, risk.

defeasance Termination of debt by an issuer. Bonds can be defeased in several ways, among them prerefunding of U.S. Government securities through an escrow account. *See also* prerefunding.

defensive industry An industry that is among those least affected by changes in the business cycle. Most defensive industries produce nondurable consumer goods, such as food and beverages, pharmaceuticals and health care, household and personal products, and energy and utilities. Public consumption remains high during periods of inflation or recession, but during inflationary periods and bull markets, defensive stocks have lower growth and return. Their strength is during recessionary periods and bear markets, when they decline less than other stocks. Defensive industry stocks have less risk but also less opportunity for high return on investment.

deferred compensation plan A contractual agreement between an employer and an employee where a portion of the employee's current compensation is paid at a later date; for example, at retirement, disability, or death. The deferred compensation is not taxed until it is paid, which may lower the employee's current tax liability.

deflation A measurable fall in prices of goods and services caused by a reduction in the supply of money or credit. Spending slows down at all levels: government, investment, and personal. Deflation usually occurs during a recession, when unemployment is increasing.

delivery vs. payment (DVP) A decision that must be made whenever a new account is opened; all new accounts must include payment and delivery instructions. Some accounts, especially large institutional accounts, are set up to handle delivery of securities and cash payments similar to cash on delivery (COD) accounts. When a client purchases a stock, the stock certificate is physically delivered to the custodian bank in exchange for payment; when the client sells the stock, the stock is delivered to the brokerage firm in exchange for payment. DVP instructions must be set up and verified before the first transaction, and the customer must notify the bank before each transaction.

demand deposit Money in commercial bank accounts that the customer can withdraw at any time. *See also* time deposit.

depreciation Loss in value of capital assets, such as equipment and machinery, with use over time. For currency, depreciation is the decline in value relative to other currencies.

depression A part of the business cycle characterized by an extended period of falling prices, high unemployment, reduced purchasing power, numerous bankruptcies, and decreased business activity. A depression is more severe than a recession. It is marked by an excess of goods produced and the consumer's inability to buy them.

derivative An instrument whose value is based on the performance of an underlying security. An option contract is a derivative; the value of the contract changes with the price of the underlying stock. A futures contract is also a derivative; its value fluctuates with the market price of the underlying commodity or currency. Derivatives can be created on almost any asset that fluctuates in value, such as stocks, agricultural products, livestock, precious metals, interest rates, foreign currency exchange rates, or stock indexes. Derivatives can be conservative, such as zero coupon Treasury securities, (CATS, STRIPS, or TIGRS). Derivatives can also be used as a hedging strategy: *Example:* A multinational corporation that needs to pay for goods 12 months in the future in a foreign currency may use exchange rate futures to lock in a favorable exchange rate. Derivatives earned a bad reputation when fund managers used them to speculate on the direction of interest rates. When their guesses were wrong, their funds suffered huge losses. The most infamous case of the inappropriate use of derivatives, was the $1.6 billion bankruptcy of Orange County, California in 1994.

designated order Orders entered for a customer during the order period for a public offering by one syndicate member with the customer's instructions that another member share in the takedown. Underwriting syndicates are required to establish the priority to be given to different types of orders and inform all interested parties in writing. Usually pre-sale orders have top priority, followed by designated orders and member orders.

devaluation A decline in the official value of something; for example, a decline in the value of a currency relative to the currencies of other nations.

diagonal spread The purchase of one option and the sale of another option in the same class (calls *or* puts on the same underlying security) but with different expiration dates and strike prices. *Example:* purchase of ABC Jan 20 puts and sale of ABC March 25 puts. *See also* spread.

Diamonds® An ETF product of Dow Jones & Company that represents ownership in the 30 component stocks of the DJIA; trades on the AMEX under the symbol DIA.

dilution The effect on earnings per share if additional shares of common stock are issued, or if convertible securities, options or warrants are converted to common stock.

direct debt The percentage of debt an issuer has in notes and bonds.

direct paper Commercial paper sold directly to investors rather than through dealer firms. Examples of direct paper issuers are Commercial Credit Corporation and General Motors Acceptance Corporation (GMAC). *See also* commercial paper, dealer paper, prime paper.

direct participation program An investment that allows for flow-through of income, gains, losses, and tax benefits directly to the owners. The business itself pays no tax because the tax liability is apportioned among the investors. Most direct participation programs are organized as limited partnerships and invest in such industries as oil and gas, real estate ventures, condominium development, or agriculture. Because of changes to the tax law on passive income, direct participation programs have lost appeal.

direct rollover *See* IRA direct rollover.

discount A price below par; for example, a $1,000 bond with a current market price of $980. *See also* par, premium.

discount rate The interest rate at which member banks borrow directly from the Federal Reserve to make up a deficiency in required reserves over the very short term, often overnight. Borrowing directly from the Federal Reserve is called "going to the discount window"; the Fed does not allow banks to borrow at the discount window for profit. The discount rate is usually lower than the federal funds rate, the rate at which member banks borrow from each other.

discount window *See* discount rate.

discretionary account A brokerage account for which the client has given the firm authority to make transactions without asking for approval each time. Many firms do not allow discretionary accounts. For those that do, the NASD has strict guidelines: NASD says discretion gives the broker authority to decide the security, the number of shares, and whether to buy or sell, but it does not apply to the timing or price of the investment. Any orders entered for a discretionary account must be marked as such. Branch office managers or other principals must approve each discretionary order and review all discretionary accounts regularly to detect orders that are excessive in size or frequency. Clients who want discretionary accounts must sign a limited trading authorization. *See also* trading authorization.

disintermediation The flow of money from low-yielding accounts at commercial and savings banks into higher-yielding investments in the marketplace; it usually occurs when the Federal Reserve tightens the money supply and interest rates rise.

diversification Management of risk by purchasing a variety of investments. Portfolios can be diversified using a number of strategies, including
* types of investments (stocks, bonds)
* sectors (stocks in a variety of industries and a variety of companies within an industry)
* geography (stocks of located both within and outside the U.S.)
* length of maturity (bond ladders).

Diversification protects investors against many forms of risk, such as bankruptcy, default, deregulation, or natural disasters. Mutual funds are the most common way for investors to diversify. *See also* risk.

diversified investment company A company that meets the 75-5-10 test of the Investment Act of 1940:
* 75 percent of total assets invested in securities issued by companies other than itself or its affiliates;
* no more than five percent of assets invested in the securities of a single corporation;
* no more than ten percent of the common stock of any single corporation owned by the investment company.

Example: For a mutual fund with $100 million in assets, at least $75 million (75 percent) must be invested in publicly traded companies; no more than $5 million (five percent) may be invested in any one corporation; and if the fund managers want to invest in a corporation with assets of $10 million, the most they may purchase is $1 million ($10 million x 10%). *See also* nondiversified investment company.

divided account *See* Western Account.

dividend Distribution of a company's net profits to shareholders, in the form of cash, stock, company products, property, or scrip. Dividends are usually paid quarterly, but the board of directors must vote to approve each payment. *See also* cash dividend, declaration date, ex-dividend date, payable date, record date, stock dividend, property dividend.

dividend payout ratio A measure of the proportion of earnings on common stock that is paid in dividends on that stock; the complement to the retained earnings ratio. *See also* retained earnings ratio.

$$\frac{\text{Annual dividends per common share}}{\text{Earnings per share}} = \text{Dividend payout ratio}$$

dividend reinvestment plan (DRIP) Use of cash dividends to purchase additional shares of a mutual fund or common stock rather than receiving the dividend in cash. Most mutual funds also allow reinvestment of capital gains.

dividend per share The dollar amount of cash dividends paid in one year on each share of common stock.

$$\frac{\text{Annual dividend}}{\text{Number of common shares outstanding}} = \text{Dividend per share}$$

dividend yield The annual rate of return an investor receives from either common or preferred stock, calculated as follows:

$$\frac{\text{Annual dividend}}{\text{Purchase price}} = \text{Dividend yield}$$

Example: A shareholder bought 100 shares of stock for $5,000; the annual dividend is $4 per share, so the dividend yield is:

$$\frac{\$400}{\$5,000} = 8\%$$

DK *See* don't know.

DNR *See* do not reduce (DNR) order.

dollar cost averaging A method of investing in which fixed-dollar amounts of stocks or mutual funds are bought at regular intervals. When prices are low, the amount buys more shares, when prices are high, fewer. In a fluctuating market, the average cost with this method is lower than if a constant number shares were purchased. *See also* constant dollar plan, constant ratio plan.

Dollar Cost Averaging

Month	Amount	Price per Share	Number of Shares
January	$500	$22	22.727
February	$500	$21	23.809
March	$500	$23	21.739
April	$500	$24	20.833
May	$500	$25	20.000
	$2,500	$23 average	109.108

donor The person making a gift of cash or securities to a child through an account opened under the UTMA. The donor may be custodian of the account or may designate another adult. *Example:* Mary Smith makes a gift of cash to her granddaughter, Amy Smith, and names her son, Michael Smith, as custodian; the title of the account would be

Michael Smith as Custodian for

Amy Smith

(Name of State) Uniform Transfer to Minors Act

Mary has no control over the account; she may not buy or sell securities or withdraw funds. If she had named herself as custodian, she would be able to manage the account.

do not reduce (DNR) order An order in the specialist's order book stating that the price in the book will not be adjusted on the ex-dividend date. Some orders are reduced in price when the stock trades ex-dividend, especially orders entered below the market, such as buy limit, sell stop, and sell stop limit. Prices on DNR orders will not be reduced for cash dividends, but will be reduced for stock distributions. *Example:* A specialist has an order to sell 100 shares of Ethan Allen at $35 stop. On ex-dividend date, October 8, the price on the order will be reduced by the amount of the dividend, $0.10, to $34.90, unless the client has requested that the order be marked DNR.

don't know (DK) A statement that the trades in a transaction do not match up. For each securities transaction, both parties send Uniform Comparison or Confirmation forms; any discrepancies are corrected, and the transactions are ready to settle with transfer of cash and securities. When the trades do not match up in CUSIP number, selling price, number of shares, or total dollar amount, the confirming broker-dealer will ask that the other dealer either confirm or DK the trade within four business days. For example, it may be that the seller sold preferred stock but tried to deliver common stock to the buyer. If the discrepancy cannot be resolved, the selling broker-dealer will disown the transaction, and the client's broker will receive a DK notice.

DOT (Designated Order Turnaround) *See* SuperDot.

double-auction market A system in which buyers enter competitive bids and sellers enter competitive offers simultaneously. The NYSE and AMEX operate double-auction markets.

double-barreled bond Bonds that have characteristics of both municipal general obligation (GO) and revenue bonds. Double-barreled bonds are backed by the taxing authority of the municipality but interest and principal are paid by revenues of the facility. Double-barreled bonds are rated and trade as GOs.

Dow Jones & Company Publisher of financial and business information through the *Wall Street Journal, Barron's*, and the *Dow Jones Indexes*. The Dow Jones averages are among the most widely quoted and oldest indices in the United States. The best known Dow Jones averages are:

Index Name	Components
Dow Jones Industrial Average	30 stocks
Transportation Average	20 stocks
Utilities Average	15 stocks
Composite Average	65 stocks from the above three averages

Dow Jones now has over 3,000 indexes available for licensing. *For more information:* www.djindexes.com and www.dowjones.com.

Dow Jones Industrial Average (DJIA) The oldest and most widely quoted index, made up of 30 of the large American industrial companies, which represent approximately 20 percent of the market value of the stocks trading on the NYSE. The component stocks are chosen by the editors of the *Wall Street Journal* for their stability and long history of growth. The 30 component stocks are:

3M Co.	Honeywell International Inc.
Alcoa Inc.	Intel Corp.
Altria Group Inc.	International Business Machines Corp.
American Express Co.	J.P. Morgan Chase & Co.
American International Group Inc.	Johnson & Johnson
Boeing	McDonald's Corp.
Caterpillar Inc.	Merck & Co. Inc.
Citigroup Inc.	Microsoft Corp.
Coca-Cola Co.	Pfizer Inc.
E.I.DuPont de Nemours & Co.	Procter & Gamble Co.
Exxon Mobil Corp.	SBC Communications Inc.
General Electric Co.	United Technologies Corp.
General Motors Corp.	Verizon Communications Inc.
Hewlett-Packard Co.	Wal-Mart Stores, Inc.
Home Depot Inc.	Walt Disney Co.

downtick *See* minus tick.

downward trendline *See* trendline.

Dow Theory The theory that major changes in the stock market must be confirmed by both the DJIA and the Dow Jones Transportation Average. Though the theory is named for Charles Dow, creator of the DJIA, there is not much evidence that he invented it.

DRIP *See* dividend reinvestment plan.

dual-purpose fund A closed-end fund that offers two types of shares: income and growth. An investor who chooses income shares receives interest and dividends from the income portfolio; the investor who chooses growth shares receives capital gains from the growth portfolio. The two types of shares are listed separately in stock quotes. A dual-purpose fund allows an investor to choose the appropriate investment objective.

due bill A statement that a seller must deliver cash, securities, or rights to the purchaser. Often stocks are sold too close to the ex-dividend date for the issuer's records to be changed. The seller is obligated to deliver the stock or cash dividend to the buyer.

due diligence In the underwriting of new issues, the process of research into the company's background, finances, management, and future plans. Underwriters often hold regional due diligence meetings, where research analysts and institutional brokers can meet with corporate managers to ask questions to determine the stability of the company.

Dutch auction A method of bidding on securities, used in buying U.S. Treasury securities, where the price starts high and is lowered until someone bids at that price.

DVP *See* delivery vs. payment (DVP).

earned income Wages, salary, tips, commissions, and net earnings from self-employment. Earned income does not include nontaxable employee benefits, such as deferred compensation, pretax dependent care benefits, or pretax medical care benefits. *See also* unearned income.

earned surplus *See* retained earnings.

earnings per share (EPS) The most popular ratio used by investors, showing the amount of profit allocated to each share of common stock. EPS is sometimes called primary earnings per share to distinguish it from earnings per share after dilution. It is calculated as follows:

Net income - Preferred stock dividends = Earnings available to common stock

$$\frac{\text{Earnings available to common stock}}{\text{Number of common shares outstanding}} = \text{Earnings per share}$$

earnings per share fully diluted A projection of EPS as if all convertible securities, outstanding rights, warrants, stock options, convertible preferred stock, or convertible bonds have been converted to common stock. The formula is the same, but the number of shares outstanding would be much larger.

Eastern account (*also called* an undivided account) A method of underwriting securities issues in which members of the underwriting syndicate act severally and jointly, which means that all firms share the risk of unsold shares. If shares cannot be sold, each firm pays a proportionate amount of their value. *Example:* An underwriter is responsible for selling 15 percent of a new issue. Some shares or bonds remain unsold. That underwriter is responsible for 15 percent of the unsold portion. *See also* Western account.

ECN *See* electronic communications network.

economic indicator A factor within the economy that can be measured and analyzed to predict the movement of the business cycle. In 1995 the Department of Commerce selected The Conference Board to collect and analyze data and publish monthly indexes of leading, coincident, and lagging indicators. The Conference Board has added business cycle indicators with additional data. Indexes of economic indicators are closely watched for trends in the business cycle. *See also* business cycle indicator, coincident indicator, lagging indicator, leading indicator.

economic risk The possibility of foreign currency devaluation or substantial changes in interest rates. Economic risk can be international or domestic and may affect entire markets. For example, the markets react strongly when the Federal Reserve signals a change in its policy on inflation and interest rates. *See also* risk.

EDGAR Electronic Data Gathering, Analysis, and Retrieval, a free electronic filing service available to all publicly traded companies. *For more information,* see the SEC's EDGAR web site, www.sec.gov/edgar/searchedgar/webusers.htm *See also* Form 8-K, Form 10-K, Form 10-Q.

education IRA *See* Coverdell educational savings account.

EE savings bond *See* Series EE bond.

efficient market theory The theory that it is impossible to beat the market, because stock prices have already factored in all relevant information.

electronic communications network (ECN) (*also called* the fourth market) A computer system that allows market makers to trade between themselves without having to go through an exchange so that network members can trade large blocks of securities directly and anonymously, off the floor of an exchange, during after-market hours, and without paying third-party commissions. *See also* Instinet, Island.

eligible security *See* marginable security.

emerging market A developing country, such as China, Brazil, and members of the former Soviet Union. Investing in companies in emerging markets is risky, but the potential reward may be higher.

Employee Retirement Income Security Act *See* ERISA.

endorsement The signature of all registered owners on the back of a stock certificate or on a stock power. The certificate or stock power must be endorsed to transfer ownership.

EPS *See* earnings per share.

equity A client's net worth in a margin account. It represents cash and securities owned minus what is owed to the brokerage firm. *See also* margin.

equity option A put or call with an underlying security of common stock. *See also* option.

equity security An investment that represents ownership in a company, such as common and preferred stocks. By contrast, bonds are debt securities that represent loans.

ERISA (Employee Retirement Income Security Act) A federal law designed to protect participants in private retirement plans from plan mismanagement and to ensure equitable participation of employees. ERISA requires that funds contributed to the plan be segregated from other corporate assets, that participants be entitled to the entire amount of their benefits within a certain period of time (vesting), that the retirement plan be in writing and be provided to participants, and that there be a procedure for grievance and appeals by participants. Amendments to ERISA include COBRA (Consolidated Omnibus Budget Reconciliation Act), and HIPAA (Health Insurance Portability and Accountability Act), both of which protect health insurance benefits for workers and their families when they change or lose their jobs.

escheat The process of turning over abandoned assets to the state. Examples of unclaimed property are cash from bank accounts, stocks, bonds, dividends, interest, insurance proceeds, contents of safe deposit boxes, or property of a person who died intestate. Brokerage firms are required to turn over cash or securities of customers for whom they have no current address to the state in which the client lived. Individuals or heirs may claim the property by applying to the state.

ETF *See* exchange-traded fund (ETF).

euro On January 1, 1999, 11 founding member countries of the European Union adopted the euro as their common currency. Beginning January 1, 2002, the European Central Bank began replacing the national currencies with the euro. The euro is now the currency of 12 EU countries: Austria, Belgium, Finland, France, Germany, Greece, Ireland, Italy, Luxembourg, the Netherlands, Portugal, and Spain.

Eurobond A major source of capital for many foreign governments and multinational corporations. Unlike the U.S. bond market, the Eurobond market is self-regulated. Bonds are in bearer form, with no registration information on the certificates. Interest payments to investors are tax-free. For those reasons, Eurobonds are not approved for sale to investors in the United States.

Eurocurrency Any currency deposited in a bank outside its country of origin, such as Japanese yen deposited in a bank in New York, or Swiss francs on deposit in London.

Eurodollar A U.S. dollar deposited in a bank outside the United States, such as in Brussels. Eurodollar deposits may be placed in any foreign bank, or any foreign branch office of a U.S. bank.

European option An option that may be exercised only during a specified period of time immediately before the expiration date. *See also* American option.

excess equity An increase in the price and market value of securities that creates additional net worth in a margin account. Excess equity may be used to buy more stock or may be withdrawn as cash. *See also* margin, special memorandum account (SMA).

exchange A place where securities are traded. U.S. exchanges are regulated by the Securities Exchange Act of 1934. Well known U.S. exchanges are the AMEX, the BSE, the CBOE, the NYSE, the PSE, and the PHLX. Many kinds of securities are traded on exchanges: stocks, bonds, rights, warrants, options, and commodities. Securities traded on an exchange must meet the listing requirements of that exchange. *See also* listed security.

exchange acquisition *See* exchange distribution.

exchange distribution A type of block trade involving several NYSE-member firms. *Example:* One firm that has a block of stock to sell asks one or two other firms to help find buyers. Once buyers are found, the firms take them to the floor and cross the trades. Exchange distributions take place during market hours, but no advance notice of the trade is given, and the trade is reported after completion. In an exchange *acquisition*, the originating firm wishes to purchase shares and asks other firms to help find sellers. *See also* block trade.

exchange market *See* exchange.

exchange privilege The right to convert shares of one mutual fund for shares of another in the same family of funds without incurring a sales charge. *Example:* A shareholder wants to exchange $10,000 of XYZ Income Fund for $10,000 of XYZ Money Market Fund. To qualify as an exchange, the investment must remain within the same family of funds and the dollar amount must be the same on the sell and buy side. In lieu of a new sales charge, the fund may charge a small exchange fee. Many funds allow clients to enter exchange instructions by telephone or the Internet. Exchanges within the same family of funds are considered sales and may be subject to capital gains taxes. *See also* mutual fund switch.

exchange-traded fund (ETF) A group of securities that tracks an index or industry sector. ETFs are unit investment trusts that trade like stocks. Over 120 ETFs trade on the AMEX, including Diamonds®, QQQ (Nasdaq 100), SPDRs (Standard & Poor's 500), and Holdrs, which represent ownership in a number of industry sectors. *See also* unit investment trust.

ex-dividend date The date on which the NASD determines the stock will trade without the dividend. *Example:* A stock trading at $50 will pay a dividend of 25 cents per share. At the opening on ex-dividend date the price of the stock will be marked down by the amount of the dividend to $49.75 per share. A stock trading ex-dividend is marked with an x in newspaper quotes. Ex-dividend date is usually two business days before the record date. *Example:* On March 1 the board of directors of LMN Corporation declared a cash dividend of 15 cents per share to shareholders of record on March 15, payable on March 30. Based on the record date of March 15, the NASD sets the ex-dividend date at March 11, two business days earlier.

March						
Sun	Mon	Tue	Wed	Thu	Fri	Sat
	1	2	3	4	5	6
7	8	9	10	11	12	13
14	15	16	17	18	19	20
21	22	23	24	25	26	27
28	29	30	31			

An investor who buys the stock *before* March 11 will be entitled to the dividend because her name will be on the books of the corporation on March 15, even if the trade settles on that day. If she buys *on or after* March 11, the investor *will not* be entitled to the next dividend. The seller will receive the dividend.

In the case of cash settlements, which settle the same day, the ex-dividend date is the day after record date.

Stock dividends may be handled differently from cash dividends. Ex-dividend date is usually the first business day after the payable date. If an investor should sell before the ex-dividend date, the sale includes an obligation to deliver to the buyer any shares obtained as a result of the dividend. A due bill is attached to the cash or securities, and the seller must deliver to the buyer.

The *Standard & Poor's Dividend Record* is a good source of cash and stock dividend information.

Bonds do not have ex-dividend or record dates. Bond interest accrues daily and is calculated and billed on trade confirmation. *See also* accrued interest, record date.

executor The person named in a decedent's will to manage the affairs of the estate. If a client dies who has an individual account or a tenants-in-common account, all open orders must be cancelled. The executor should provide the brokerage firm with a death certificate and a copy of the legal document appointing the executor. The executor will give instructions as to the disposition of the account.

exempt security Securities exempt from SEC registration requirements and Regulation T (Reg T): stocks and bonds that are not regulated by SEC and Federal Reserve rules, such as Treasury bills, notes, and bonds; government agency securities; municipal securities; and non-convertible corporate bonds. Exempt securities may be purchased on margin without Reg T minimum requirements, but NYSE, NASD, and house margin criteria determine loan value. *See also* margin, blue-sky laws.

exercise Use of an option to buy or sell the underlying security at the price specified in the option contract. An option contract is worth exercising if it is in the money, for example, a General Electric June 30 call when the current price of GE is $35 or an eBay April 65 put when the current price of eBay is $60. *See also* in-the-money, option.

exercise price (*also called the* strike price) The price at which the owner of an option contract will be entitled to buy the underlying security and the seller of the contract must deliver the security. In the case of a Microsoft April $27.50 call, $27.50 is the exercise price.

ex-legal A municipal bond certificate without the legal opinion and so stamped. If not so stamped, the legal opinion, which is required by MSRB rules, must be printed on or attached to the bond certificate; it addresses the validity of the bond offering and its tax-exempt status.

expansion (*also known as* recovery) The part of the business cycle when business activity increases. Typical indicators of expansion are increasing production, rising stock markets, increased demand for goods and services, rising property values, increasing and gross national product. *See also* business cycle.

expiration cycle Group of expiration months for equity, commodity and currency options. Cycles are January, April, July, October (JAJO); February, May, August, November (FMAN); and March, June, September, December (MJSD). If Microsoft has options expiring in January, April, July and October, the OCC will create new options on expiration of the October options. In addition to the quarterly cycles, options are always available on the current month and the following month. Equity LEAPS expire in January of every year. Index LEAPS expire in January and December of every year.

expiration date The date on which a listed option must either be exercised or become worthless. Equity options expire on the Saturday immediately following the third Friday of the expiration month.

extension *See* Regulation T extension

extraordinary call Early, unexpected redemption of a bond because a project is cancelled, perhaps because of a natural disaster, such as a flood, or because not enough bonds were sold to fund the project. *See also* catastrophe call.

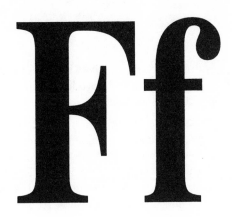

face-amount certificate A debt security sold by investment companies. Investors can make lump sum or periodic payments to buy the certificates at a discount. At maturity, they receive the face value of the certificate. Changes to tax laws have made face-amount certificates nearly obsolete. *See also* investment company.

face value (*also called* par value, principal) The value of a bond or note at maturity. The price of a corporate bond issued, as is usual, with a $1,000 face value will fluctuate over the life of the bond as interest rates change, but it will be redeemed at $1,000.

fail to deliver The failure of the broker-dealer on the sale side of a transaction to send securities in good delivery to the broker-dealer on the buy side. Until the securities are delivered, the seller may not be paid the proceeds of the transaction. If after ten days the selling broker-dealer has not delivered the securities to the buyer, the buyer may execute a buy-in to complete the trade and charge the selling broker-dealer, regardless of the price. *See also* good delivery.

fail to receive The failure of a broker-dealer to be given securities in good order to settle a trade. *See also* good delivery.

Fannie Mae *See* Federal National Mortgage Association.

feasibility study The determination of a potential revenue bond issuer's estimated costs and revenues associated with a project and identification of any competing enterprises before the issue is brought to the market. *See also* due diligence.

The Fed *See* Federal Reserve.

fed call *See* Regulation T call.

Federal Farm Credit Bank Financial institutions that are part of the Farm Credit System (FCS). They offer credit to farmers and ranchers using funding from the sale of short-term discount notes and Federal Farm Credit Bank Consolidated Systemwide Securities, which are six- and nine-month notes and longer-term bonds.

federal funds The minimum reserves as a percentage of deposits that the Federal Reserve requires commercial banks to maintain, which are deposited at a Federal Reserve Bank. *Example:* The reserve requirement is ten percent. Member banks must deposit $10 at the Federal Reserve for every $100 in transaction deposits that it holds. The remaining $90 is available for loan to other member banks needing to meet their reserve requirements. Many large banks loan out more than they take in in deposits, and often need to borrow funds overnight to meet the reserve requirements. Federal funds redistribute bank reserves and allow surplus reserves to earn interest. Institutions that participate in the federal funds market are commercial banks, branches of foreign banks in the U.S., and government securities dealers.

federal funds rate The interest rate at which Federal Reserve member banks borrow from each other over the very short term, often overnight. The federal funds rate is usually higher than the discount rate at which member banks borrow directly from the Fed. *See also* open market operations.

Federal Home Loan Mortgage Corporation (FHLMC) (*also known as* Freddie Mac) A publicly-held corporation that buys home mortgages from financial institutions, repackages them as a pool, and resells them as pass-through mortgage securities. One type, mortgage participation certificates (PCs) passes principal and interest payments to investors monthly. A second type, guaranteed mortgage certificates (GMCs) pays interest semiannually and principal annually.

Federal National Mortgage Association (FNMA) (*also known as* Fannie Mae) A publicly held corporation that buys mortgages from the FHA and the VA, repackages them, and sells them to investors. In addition to mortgage-backed securities, FNMA issues notes and bonds, and investors can also buy FNMA's common stock.

Federal Open Market Committee (FOMC) A policy-making arm of the Federal Reserve. The FOMC has 12 members: the seven members of the Board of Governors of the Federal Reserve System, the president of the Federal Reserve Bank of New York, and four of the other 11 Federal Reserve Bank presidents, who serve one-year terms on a rotating basis. The FOMC holds eight regular meetings each year and meets more often if needed. Since January 2000, the FOMC has issued a statement after each meeting outlining its assessment of risk to its long-term goal of price stability and economic growth. The FOMC uses open market operations to control the money supply by setting a target level for the federal funds rate. If the Fed wants to expand the money supply, the FOMC purchases U.S. Treasury securities in the open market. This increases the money in the banking system, stimulates growth, and puts downward pressure on the federal funds rate. Sales of Treasury securities by the FOMC in the open market have the opposite effect, decreasing the availability of bank reserves and forcing interest rates higher. *See also* open market operations.

Federal Reserve (*also known as* the Fed) The central bank of the United States. The Fed is an independent corporation under the direction of Congress. Its duties are to: (1) conduct U.S. monetary policy, (2) supervise and regulate banking institutions and the credit rights of their customers, (3) maintain stability in the financial system, and (4) provide financial services to the U.S. government, financial institutions, the public, and foreign official institutions. For an excellent overview of the Federal Reserve's history and operations, *see* www.FederalReserveEducation.org.

Federal Reserve Bank A regional operating arm of the Federal Reserve System in one of its 12 districts.

Federal Reserve Board The Board of Governors responsible for setting U.S. monetary policy. The Fed Board, which has seven members, uses three tools to control the money supply: open market operations, the discount rate, and reserve requirements. *See also* discount rate, federal funds rate, open market operations, reserve requirement.

FHLMC *See* Federal Home Loan Mortgage Corporation.

fidelity bond An insurance policy against losses due to employee dishonesty, such as check forgery, lost securities, or fraudulent trading. Brokerage firms that are members of SIPC, NASD, or the exchanges must maintain blanket fidelity coverage.

fiduciary A person or company appointed to act on behalf of another person in managing that person's account, such as a custodian of a minor's account, a trustee, the executor of an estate, or a guardian. Fiduciaries have no ownership in the assets in an account.

fiduciary account An account in which the assets are held for the beneficial interest of the owner, but the owner does not control the account; another person, such as a custodian, acts in the best interests of the owner. The title of the account must show the relationship between fiduciary and beneficial owner, for example, James Brown as Custodian for William Brown, or John Smith, Trustee for the Robert Smith Trust.

The beneficial owner's Social Security number or tax identification number is used to open the account. For accounts other than UGMA/UTMA custodial accounts, legal documentation (a copy of a trust or court order) must be provided showing that the fiduciary is authorized to manage the account. For custodial accounts, no legal documentation is required. Fiduciaries must act prudently for the beneficial owners. For that reason, margin accounts may not be opened unless they are specifically allowed in the legal documents establishing the account. Option trading is generally prohibited.

FIFO *(first-in, first-out)* The accounting rule that if a number of identical items, such as shares of stock, are purchased at different times, the sale of any of them is automatically the sale of the first lot purchased. When investors sell stock and do not indicate at the time of sale which lot is being sold, the IRS will use the FIFO rule. An investor who wants to offset some gains by selling a lot purchased later should clearly identify the lot being sold at the time of sale. Clients who hold stock certificates should deliver the lot to be sold to their broker, or if shares are held in street name, ask that the broker identify the lot being sold on the sale confirmation. *Example:* If a customer is selling 200 shares of stock, the broker should add a notation "100 shares purchased 4/1/1990, 100 shares purchased 11/6/1992" to the sell order so it will appear on the confirmation. *See also* LIFO.

fill-or-kill (FOK) order An instruction for the broker to immediately fill the order or the entire order is cancelled. *Example*: A floor broker has an order to buy 1000 Wal-Mart at $56. A broker from another firm has 500 shares for sale at $56. If the floor broker had an FOK order, the entire order must be canceled because the entire 1000 shares is not available for sale. *See also* immediate-or-cancel order.

final prospectus *See* prospectus.

Financial Services Modernization Act of 1999 *See* Gramm-Leach-Bliley Act.

financial planner An adviser providing services similar to an investment advisor, but also able to give advice on an individual's total financial situation, including insurance, taxes, and estate planning. *See also* certified financial planner (CFP).

financial risk The probability of losing part or all of an investment due to the failure of the issuer. *See also* bond rating, risk.

firm commitment An underwriting agreement in which underwriters and issuer sign a letter of intent in which the underwriters agree to buy the securities being issued and set an approximate date of purchase and a price range. If part of an issue cannot be sold, the loss is distributed among the underwriters according to their percentage of participation. *See also* underwriting agreement.

firm quote The price in the interdealer market at which a broker-dealer is ready to buy or sell at least one round lot (100 shares) of stock or five bonds. All quotes are considered firm unless indicated otherwise. See also nominal quote, subject quote, workout quote.

first in, first out *See* FIFO.

fiscal policy The planning by Congress and the President of the government's spending and revenue-producing activities. Using money raised though taxes and federal spending, the government can reduce or increase the rate of inflation to influence economic growth. *See also* monetary policy.

fixed asset Property that is not consumed or converted to cash, such as buildings, machinery and equipment, furniture, and fixtures. Fixed assets on a balance sheet are often shown at their depreciated value.

fixed income security An investment, such as a bond or preferred stock, with a predetermined dividend or interest payment. The amount of the dividend is carried in the description. *Example:* An AT&T 6% bond will pay $60 for every $1,000 invested, every year until maturity; a $6 preferred stock will pay $6 per share every year.

flat yield curve *See* yield curve.

floor broker (*also called* commission house broker) A trader on the floor of an exchange who executes trades for a brokerage firm's clients and for the firm's own accounts.

flower bond Unique Treasury bonds, not issued since 1971 (the last issue matured in 1998), that were issued at a discount and redeemed after the owner's death to pay federal estate taxes.

flow of funds The order in which the issuer of a revenue bond promises to pay expenses from income produced by the facility funded by the issue. The flow of funds is usually outlined in the feasibility statement. The issuer uses either a gross revenue pledge, where debt service is paid first, or a net revenue pledge, where operating and maintenance expenses are paid first.

FNMA *See* Federal National Mortgage Association.

FOK *See* fill or kill.

FOMC *See* Federal Open Market Committee.

forced conversion An action taken by issuers of convertible securities, which cannot force owners to convert, but can make the situation too attractive to resist. Most convertible securities, such as bonds and preferred stocks, are callable. If the parity price is higher than the call price, owners would benefit by converting to common stock rather than to submit the securities for redemption. *See also* conversion parity, convertible security.

foreign exchange rate The rate at which the currency of one country is converted to the currency of another country. Exchange rates change daily. *Example:* A currency quotation for Canadian dollars lists two rates: U.S. equivalent (.6871) and Currency per U.S. dollar (1.4554). One Canadian dollar would buy $0.6871 U.S.; one U.S. dollar would buy $1.4554 Canadian.

Form 8-K *See* 8-K

Form 10-K *See* 10-K.

Form 10-Q *See* 10-Q.

forward pricing The practice of holding a written request for redemption of mutual funds until the next NAV calculation and then redeeming the shares. A mutual fund's NAV must be calculated at least once each business day. Most funds calculate their NAV after the close of each market session. Mutual funds are required to base all new purchase and redemption orders on the *next* NAV.

fourth market The market in which institutional investors buy and sell securities from each other without going through a broker. A dealer firm, Instinet, matches orders directly through a computer system. In this system, buyers and sellers remain anonymous, and large commissions or markups are avoided. *See also* Instinet, Island.

fractional share Any amount of corporate ownership that is less than one whole share. Mutual fund shares and reinvested dividends are credited in fractional shares. *Example:* An investment of $12,000 in a no-load mutual fund with an NAV of $15.375 will buy 780.488 shares. A cash dividend of $50 reinvested will buy .694 shares of a stock priced at $72 per share. Fractional shares are not commonly distributed to clients. If a fractional share is credited for a stock split or dividend, the issuer will send a certificate for the full shares and a check for the cash equivalent of the fractional share.

Freddie Mac *See* Federal Home Loan Mortgage Corporation.

free credit balance *(also called a* credit register (CR)*)* Cash that a brokerage firm is holding in a client's account.

free crowd *See* active crowd.

front-end load Mutual fund sales charges added to the NAV at the time of purchase. A front-end load plus the NAV equals the public offering price (POP). Investors who pay a front-end load are not charged a sales charge at the time of redemption. *Example:* A fund's NAV is $15 per share and the fund has a load of 4.5 percent, so buyers of the fund would pay an offering price of $15.675 per share. *See also* back-end load, load.

front-running An unethical practice in which a broker-dealer has inside information about a company or has a large customer order that will probably affect the price of the stock, and the broker-dealer enters an order for its own account ahead of the client's, or fills its order at a price better than the client's. *Example:* A brokerage firm buys shares of a company's stock just before the firm announces a buy recommendation on the stock.

frozen account An account in which securities may be bought and sold, but all purchases must be on a cash-in-advance basis, and stocks must be long in the account before they can be sold. *Example:* If a client buys a security in a cash account and sells the security without paying for it (called *selling to cover*), the account is immediately frozen for a period of 90 days.

Full Disclosure Act *See* Securities Act of 1933.

full trading authorization Permission given to an appointee by an account owner to make investment decisions for the owner's account, as well as deposit or withdraw cash or securities from the account. *See also* discretionary account, limited trading authorization.

fully registered bond *See* registered bond.

fundamental analysis The study of the behavior of broad-based economic trends, such as economic indicators, and the performance of industries and individual companies. Fundamental analysts are most interested in the balance sheet of a corporation and how its stock compares with other companies in the same business. Many market analysts use both fundamental and technical analysis to support their recommendations: fundamental analysis to choose which company's stock to buy, and technical analysis for timing purchases and sales. *See also* technical analysis.

funded debt A corporate or municipal bond with a maturity of a year or more or a bond issue that has a sinking fund to pay for redemption. *See also* sinking fund.

fungibility The extent to which an asset can be replaced by something of equal value and description. *Example:* A certificate for 100 shares of Starbucks is replaceable by a new certificate for 100 shares.

futures contract A standardized agreement for the purchase or sale of a commodity at a specific price on a future date. A futures contract obligates the buyer to take delivery of the goods, and the seller to sell it, unless the contract is sold before settlement date. Many futures investors do not want to take delivery of the commodity but simply to profit from buying and selling the contract. However, futures offer farmers, ranchers, and manufacturers of processed foods a hedge against changes in the price of agricultural or livestock prices, or let a corporation lock in an exchange rate on a foreign currency for an upcoming transaction.

futures market Markets for futures contracts, which are traded on several exchanges using the open outcry system, among them the Merc, the CBOT, the Kansas City Board of Trade, the New York Futures Exchange, the International Monetary Market, and COMEX, a division of the New York Mercantile Exchange.

GDP *See* gross domestic product.

general obligation (GO) bond A type of municipal bond with the following characteristics :

- GOs are backed by the full faith and credit of the issuer.
- GOs are used to fund capital projects that do not generate revenue, such as new schools, libraries, or city office buildings.
- Principal and interest payments of GOs are financed by taxes. Local issues, such as bonds issued by cities, counties or school districts, are financed by ad valorem property taxes and local fees; state issues by income and sales taxes and state licenses and fees.
- Because they are financed by taxes, GO bonds require voter approval.
- The credit of GO bond issuers is rated by services like Moody's and Standard & Poor's.
- New issues of GO bonds are awarded to underwriters through competitive bidding.
  See also revenue bond.

gift tax A levy on gifts of cash or securities, unless they are within the exclusion limit. For 2005, gifts with a value of $11,000 to an individual or $22,000 to a married couple are exempt from gift tax.

Ginnie Mae *See* Government National Mortgage Association.

Glass-Steagall Act of 1933 (*also known as the* Banking Act) A federal law that prohibited commercial banks from engaging in investment banking, except for underwriting municipal general obligation bonds. Glass-Steagall was enacted after the crash of 1929 when Congress concluded that so many banks failed because of their role as investment bankers, using commercial deposits to under-write stock offerings. The Glass-Steagall prohibitions were repealed by the Gramm-Leach-Bliley Act in 1999. *See also* Gramm-Leach-Bliley Act of 1999.

GNMA *See* Government National Mortgage Association.

GNP *See* gross domestic product.

GO *See* general obligation bond.

going private The buy-up of shares of a publicly traded company by an individual, group of people, or organization with the intent of moving it to private ownership.

going public The new issue market, where privately owned companies raise capital by selling securities to the general public. *See also* initial public offering.

good delivery The attributes of securities certificates deposited for transfer that must be met by clients depositing securities to their brokerage accounts and broker-dealers delivering securities to each other. For securities to be in good delivery, the registered certificates must be assigned (endorsed) by all owners or must carry attached a signed stock or bond power. If certificates are registered in the name of a trust, corporation, or fiduciary account, documentation will be required to show that the person who signed the certificate is authorized to do so. Certified copies of trust agreements, court orders, or corporate resolutions may be required. All signatures must be guaranteed by an exchange-member firm or a national bank. The transfer agent is the final judge of whether securities are in good delivery.

good-till-canceled (GTC) order (*also known as* open orders) Orders that are valid until filled or canceled by the client. However, on the last business days of April and October, all GTC orders must be confirmed by the client or they will be canceled. This practice removes obsolete orders from the specialist order book and prevents execution of orders that clients have forgotten. GTC orders are limit or stop orders; market orders must not be entered GTC. *Example:* "Buy 100 Aloca at 27 GTC" means that an order to buy 100 shares of Alcoa at 27, if not executed the day it was entered, will be entered into the specialist order book and stay there until it can be filled or the client cancels the order. Where the order is confirmed semiannually, the order will not lose its original position in the specialist's book.

Government National Mortgage Association (GNMA) (*also known as* Ginnie Mae) A government-owned corporation established in 1968 within the Department of Housing and Urban Development. GNMA buys FHA and VA mortgages and auctions them to private firms, which pool the mortgages and sell pass-through certificates to investors. The principal and interest payments from the pooled mortgages pass through to investors in monthly payments. GNMAs are unique because they are guaranteed by the U.S. government.

Gramm-Leach-Bliley Act of 1999 A law that repealed portions of the Glass-Steagall Act of 1933, which had created a wall between commercial banks and securities firms. The Gramm-Leach-Bliley Act allows commercial banks and investment firms to affiliate under one holding company, under authority of the

Federal Reserve; highly-rated national banks may form new subsidiaries for the purpose of underwriting and selling securities, but not insurance, insurance company portfolio investments, or real estate development or investment; banks may engage in certain broker-dealer activities previously prohibited under Glass-Steagall. Gramm-Leach-Bliley also amends the Investment Advisors Act and Investment Company Act to allow bankers to provide investment advice. In addition, Gramm-Leach-Bliley regulates the collection and disclosure of customers' personal financial information held by financial institutions, such as banks, brokerage firms, insurance companies, credit reporting agencies, firms that prepare personal tax returns or provide credit counseling, or residential real estate settlement services. A pretexting provision protects consumers from individuals and companies that obtain personal and financial information under false pretenses *(pretexting)*; *Example:* A telemarketer makes a fraudulent offer to get credit card or bank information. *See also* Glass-Steagall Act of 1933.

green shoe *(also called an* overallotment provision) A provision in an underwriting agreement in which the issuer agrees to authorize, if there is exceptional public demand, additional shares for purchase by members of the underwriting syndicate. The name comes from the Green Shoe Company, which was the first to grant the option.

gross domestic product (GDP) The measure of the total annual output of goods and services of a country: total personal consumption, government spending, corporate production, private investments, and total exports. Reported quarterly by the Department of Commerce, GDP, formerly called the gross national product (GNP), is an indicator of the health of the economy.

gross national product *See* gross domestic product.

gross revenue pledge The promise by a revenue bond issuer to pay debt service first, with operations and maintenance expenses paid by the user from income generated by the facility. The issuer uses either a net revenue pledge, where operating and maintenance expenses are paid first, or a gross revenue pledge. *See also* flow of funds, net revenue pledge.

group net order Orders entered during the order period for new issues for which the member credits the sale to the entire syndicate instead of itself, to help ensure that the order will be filled. The takedown for the order is credited to all members of the syndicate according to participation.

growth fund A mutual fund with the investment objective of appreciating faster than the market as a whole. Growth funds may be conservative, investing in large-cap equity securities designed for long-term capital appreciation, or aggressive, with a portfolio of small, newer companies. Many growth companies invest their earnings back into the company for research and development rather than paying dividends.

growth industry Stocks of companies in sectors that are growing faster than the economy in general, such as telecommunications and information technology and services. Because most of these companies retain their profits for research and development, very few pay dividends.

GTC *See* good-till-cancelled.

guaranteed stock A stock on which the payment of dividends is guaranteed by another company. The guarantee does not apply to the value of the stock itself. The only guarantee is to the dividend, therefore it is considered a type of preferred stock. The most common industries to use guaranteed stocks are utilities and railroads.

guardian A person appointed by a court to manage the affairs of a minor until the minor reaches the age of majority or to handle the affairs of an incompetent. A court order showing appointment of that person as guardian is required to open a fiduciary brokerage account.

hedge A strategy to protect an investment at least in part by another transaction that could offset any loss in the original investment. *Examples:* An investor who is long a stock might write covered calls or buy puts. A multinational corporation with a contract to deliver materials in exchange for a foreign currency might use currency options to protect against a significant change in the exchange rate.

hedge fund A fund similar to a mutual fund that pools investors' money to make a profit. However, hedge funds are not registered with the SEC and are only lightly regulated. Hedge funds use high-risk investment strategies, such as short positions, swaps, arbitrage, and derivatives. They use program trading to move billions of dollars in and out of markets quickly. Investors in hedge funds are usually accredited investors or institutions. Minimum investments are often quite high, such as $1 million.

A fairly new investment product is the fund of hedge funds. Some funds of hedge funds register with the SEC and must give investors a prospectus and file semi-annual reports with the SEC. Some funds of hedge funds have lower investment minimums than the component hedge funds, such as $25,000, and allow nonaccredited investors to purchase them.

HH savings bond *See* Series HH bond.

high-yield bond *See* speculative bond.

HIPPA *See* ERISA.

holding period The amount of time an investor owns a security. For tax purposes, assets held one year or less bring in short-term capital gains or losses, and those more than one year bring in long-term gains or losses.

holding period return The rate of return on an investment, taking into consideration the amount of time the investor has owned the security. *Example:* An investor bought 100 shares of stock at $25, sold it at $30, and received $200 in dividends; the return is $700 ($500 capital gain + $200 dividend), or 28 percent

($700 ÷$2,500 invested). A 28 percent return is considerable if the stock was held for only a year; if the stock were held for 15 years, the return would be far from adequate.

horizontal spread *See* calendar spread.

hot issue A stock being brought to market for the first time in an IPO that is in high demand. These stocks may have immediate price gains when trading begins. In 2004, SEC Rule 2790 took effect, which prohibits exchange members firm from selling a new issue to an account in which a restricted person has a beneficial interest. Restricted persons include most associated persons of a member, and most owners and affiliates of a broker-dealer. The rule eliminates the requirement that a new issue be "hot" and it now applies to all new issues. *See also* initial public offering, sticky issue.

house requirement *See* margin.

hypothecation agreement The part of a margin agreement that gives the brokerage firm permission to use the securities as collateral for the margin loan. The firm may not pledge more securities than are needed to cover the amount of the loan. *See also* customer protection rule, margin agreement, rehypothecation.

immediate-or-cancel (IOC) order An instruction for the broker to immediately fill the order or the order is cancelled. IOC orders are similar to fill-or-kill orders, except that *partial execution is acceptable. Example*: A floor broker has an order to buy 1000 Wal-Mart at $56. A broker from another firm has 500 shares for sale at $56. If the floor broker had an IOC order, 500 shares could be filled and the rest of the order must be cancelled if no other shares are available for sale. *See also* fill-or-kill order.

inactive crowd (*also called* the cabinet crowd, can crowd) Members of the NYSE who trade inactive, infrequently traded bonds or those with low volume. Low volume and illiquidity tend to make it difficult for investors to get good prices for their bonds. *See also* active crowd.

income fund A mutual fund with an investment objective of current yield, or income. The fund may invest in common or preferred stocks of companies paying dividends, such as utilities or blue chip stocks, or in corporate, convertible, or U.S. government bonds.

income statement (*also called the* profit and loss statement) That part of a corporation's financial statement that summarizes revenues and expenses for a specific period. The income statement is a history of the company's revenues, costs, and expenses during the accounting period, which might be annual, semi-annual, quarterly, or monthly.

indefeasible title A title that cannot be made null or void. For instance, in the case of gifts or transfers to minors under UGMA or UTMA, the donor may not take back a gift, and the minor may not give back a gift until he or she has reached the age of majority. Gifts to minors are thus irrevocable.

indenture *See* trust indenture.

index An index measures the movement of the market. Indexes may be broad-based, reflecting the movement of a large part of the market, such as the Standard & Poor's 500 and the Russell 2000, or narrow-based, measuring the movement in a particular sector, such as pharmaceuticals or semiconductors. The most widely-quoted index, Dow Jones Industrial Average, measures 30 of the largest companies in the United States.

index arbitrage Arbitrage in which investors try to take advantage of differences between prices of stocks in an index and the price of a futures contract on that index. An investor might buy either the stock or a futures contract on the stock and simultaneously sell the other. Because of the high cost of buying and selling stocks and futures contracts, and the computer programs needed to track the stocks and futures contracts, index arbitrage is usually the work of money managers rather than individual investors. *See also* arbitrage, collar.

index option Calls and puts on stock indexes. The Chicago Board Options Exchange (CBOE) trades cash-settled index options on approximately 40 indexes. Each index is assigned a multiplier, such as 100, to its base value. The value of the index responds to movements in price in the component securities of the index. Cash-settled index options are thus similar to stock options. Just as stock options are defined as contracts that give the buyer the right to buy or sell a stock at a stated price for a limited period of time, so do cash-settled index options give buyers similar rights. However, the underlying asset covered by index options is not shares in a company but rather an underlying dollar value equal to the index level multiplied by $100. The amount of cash received upon exercise depends on the closing value of the index in comparison to the strike price of the index option.

Index options allow investors to make investment decisions on a specific market industry or on the market as a whole. Each index is unique and may cover a broad array of underlying stocks or only represent a narrow sector of the market.

The Chicago Board Options Exchange (CBOE) has an excellent example of an index option trade on their web site at www.cboe.com/LearnCenter/pdf/DJX-DIAbrochure.pdf. In the example, an investor who believes the DJIA will go higher and wishes to participate without a large initial cash investment, buys DJIA calls.

DJX is the symbol for options on the DJIA. DJX is based on 1/100th of the DJIA. If the DJIA were at 10,300, the options index would be 103. An investor could purchase five six-month call options with a strike price of 103. Each premium point is multiplied by $100 to determine total cost. Therefore, if you paid a premium of $5.00, you have paid $2,500 for five contracts (5.00 x 5 x $100 = $2,500). To make a profit, the DJX must rise above a break-even point of 108 (103 + 5.00 = 108).

If the DJIA reaches 11,000 at expiration (DIX = 110), the five 103 calls would be worth $3,500(110-103) x 5 x $100 = $3,500. You would then reduce this amount by the premium paid ($2,500) to arrive at a profit of $1,000.

If the DJIA falls below 10,300 at expiration (DJX = 103) your calls would expire worthless and your loss would be limited to the total premium paid of $2,500.

Index options other than Diamonds® trade on a cash-settled basis. No shares of underlying stock are bought or sold. Many index options exercise on a European-style basis: they may be exercised only on expiration date. Others exercise on an American-style basis: they may be exercised at any time before the expiration date. *See also* LEAPS; options; Diamonds.

indication of interest A statement by investors that they might be interested in buying a new issue after it is cleared by the SEC. While new securities are in the registration period, underwriters and brokers may talk to potential investors about the new issue and take indications of interest. At this point, there is no obligation to buy, because the security cannot be purchased until it clears the registration process. Clients who express an indication of interest must be sent a preliminary prospectus.

individual account A type of account with only one beneficial owner. The account holder is the only person who can control the investments in the account, and give instructions for distribution of cash or securities.

individual retirement account *See* IRA.

industrial development revenue bond (*also called* industrial development bonds, industrial revenue bonds) A bond used by a municipality to finance construction of a facility or to buy equipment, which is then leased to private persons or businesses. The municipality uses lease payments to fund interest and principal payments. The corporation leasing the facility and/or equipment is ultimately responsible for making those payments; if it defaults the municipality is not liable. The credit rating of the bond is the corporation's. However, because they are municipal bonds, interest on industrial revenue bonds is federally tax-exempt.

inflation A measurable rise in prices of goods and services. Inflation usually occurs during a period of expansion when unemployment is decreasing.

inflation risk (*also called* purchasing power risk). The type of risk that concerns the rate of inflation during the time a client's funds are invested. If the rate of inflation grows faster than the yield on an investment, the investor's money will have less purchasing power when the investment matures or is sold. *For example*, if an investor buys a $10,000 bond that pays six percent per year for 20 years, and over that 20 years inflation rises from five percent to eight percent, the client's $10,000 will buy less at the end of 20 years. *See also* risk.

initial margin requirement The amount that must be deposited in a margin account before stock can be bought. A client who buys stock in a margin account is required to deposit a certain percentage of the purchase price. The initial margin requirement is set by Regulation T (Reg. T) and is currently 50 percent or $2,000, whichever is higher. *See also* margin.

initial public offering (IPO) An offering of stock in the new issue market where privately-owned companies raise capital by selling securities to the general public. In 2004, SEC Rule 2790 took effect. Rule 2790 now prohibits exchange members from selling a new issue to an account in which a restricted person has a beneficial interest. Restricted persons include most associated persons of a member firm, most owners and affiliates of a broker-dealer. The rule eliminates the requirement that a new issue be "hot" and it now applies to all new issues. *See also* hot issue, restricted person, underwriting.

inside information "material nonpublic information" as defined by the SEC. Buying or selling securities based on such information is illegal. *See also* insider.

inside market For over-the-counter stocks, the market that has the best (highest) bid price at which a stock may be sold, and the best (lowest) ask price at which a stock may be bought at any time during the trading period. The competitive nature of the market is shown in the following. *Example:* of three securities firms making markets in XYZ Corp. stock (below), Gamma Securities has the inside market, displaying the highest bid and the lowest ask price. OTC traders wanting to buy or sell XYZ Corp. stock will go to Gamma Securities first with their XYZ orders. A trader would go to the other two firms only if Gamma Securities does not have enough stock to fill the orders.

Market Maker	Bid	Ask
Alpha Securities	40	41
Beta Securities	40.125	41
Gamma Securities	40.25	39.875

insider (*also called* affiliated person) A company's officers, directors, employees, and anyone owning more than ten percent of any class of the corporation's securities. Insiders are privy to information about the company that is not public. Because of their close connections to their companies, insiders own control stock, the sale of which is regulated by SEC Rule 144. *See also* control stock, Rule 144.

insider trading Buying and selling of the company's stock by affiliated persons. Contrary to popular belief, insider trading is legal when done through the proper channels. Insiders must file statements with the SEC disclosing purchases and sales, and this information is reported to the public. The Sarbanes-Oxley Act of 2002 accelerated the filing dates of these disclosures.

The SEC describes illegal insider trading as "buying or selling a security, in breach of a fiduciary duty or other relationship of trust and confidence, while in possession of material, nonpublic information about the security" (SEC). Public knowledge of such information could cause a stock's price to rise or fall dramatically. Illegal activities include disseminating nonpublic information to someone else; securities trading by the person who received such information; and securities trading by those who misappropriate such information.

Insider Trading and Securities Fraud Enforcement Act of 1988 Amendment to the Securities Exchange Act of 1934 that expands the liabilities and penalties for illegal insider trading, and gives legal recourse to investors who lose money in their investments due to insider trading violations. The Act allows the SEC to levy penalties of up to three times the profit made in illegal inside trading. It applies not only to people who buy and sell based on insider information, but also to those people who disseminate nonpublic information.

Instinet ECN (*also called the* fourth market) An ECN founded in 1969, Instinet is an affiliate of Instinet Group Incorporated, a broker-dealer whose clients are institutional investors and mutual funds. Linked by computer, Instinet's subscribers are able to trade large blocks of securities directly and anonymously, off the floor of an exchange, during after-market hours, and without paying third-party commissions. *See also* electronic communications networks (ECNs), fourth market.

institutional investor An institutional investor is an organization that buys and sells large quantities of securities. Examples of institutional investors include mutual funds, banks, and retirement plans.

interdealer network The over-the-counter market, where trading takes place by computer and phone, by registered broker-dealer firms that buy and sell securities for their own accounts and for their clients. Broker-dealers post their best bid and offer prices and buy and sell from each other. By contrast, the NYSE and AMEX are exchanges which conduct double-auction markets.

interest (1) The cost of borrowing money, usually stated as an annual rate. Bond issuers pay interest to investors, usually semi-annually. *Example:* an investor who owns a $10,000 bond paying five percent due 1/1/2020 will receive interest of $250.00 every six months.

(2) Shows the amount of ownership a stockholder has in a company, expressed as a percentage. *Example:* an investor who owns 10,000 shares of a company with 100,000 shares outstanding owns a ten percent interest in the company.

interest coverage ratio A ratio that helps bondholders determine if a corporation has adequate earnings to cover its bond interest payments. It measures the number of times earnings before interest and taxes (EBIT) exceeds annual interest on the company's outstanding bonds. The formula is:

$$\frac{\text{EBIT}}{\text{annual interest payable to bondholders}} = \text{interest coverage ratio}$$

interest rate The cost of using or borrowing money, expressed as a percentage. *See also* broker call rate, discount rate, federal funds rate, prime rate.

interest rate option An option contract that has a U.S. Treasury security as its underlying security. Investors who have opinions on the direction of interest rates may trade interest rate options. The buyer of an interest rate call believes interest rates will go up; a put buyer expects interest rates to go down. Interest rate options are cash-settled, European-style, and trade on the Chicago Board Options Exchange (CBOE). They are available on the 13-week T-bill, 5-year T-note, 10-year T-note, and 30-year T-bond. Options on the 13-week T-bill are based on the discount rate of the most recently auctioned 13-week T-bill. The new T-bill is substituted each week following its auction. The 5-year T-note, 10-year T-note, and 30-year T-bond options are based on ten times the yield to maturity on the most recently auctioned 5-year T-note, 10-year T-note, and 30-year T-bonds, respectively. LEAPS are also available on interest rate options. *See also* LEAPS, options.

interest rate risk The possibility that interest rates will change during the time an investor owns a fixed-income investment. *Example:* If an investor owns a 20-year four percent bond, and interest rates rise during the life of the bond, the investor will lose earnings potential and the value of the bond will decline due to the change in interest rates. *See also* risk.

international arbitrage Arbitrage in which investors try to take advantage of inconsistencies between American and foreign stock markets, ADRs and foreign stocks, or currency exchange rates. *See also* arbitrage.

interpolation A method used to determine price or yield of a bond from a bond table when the price or yield falls between two numbers in the table. The new yield and price will be the same percentage above or below the numbers in the table. *See also* bond basis book.

in-the-money An option contract on a stock whose current market price is higher than the strike price of a call option, or lower than the strike price of a put option. *Examples:* A General Electric June 30 call is in the money if the current market price of GE is $35. Much the same, an eBay April 65 put is in the money if the current price of eBay is $60. *See also* at-the-money, out-of-the-money, breakeven point.

intrinsic value The worth of an option that is in-the-money. A call option has intrinsic value when its strike price is below the current market price, a put option has intrinsic value when its strike price is above the current market price. The amount of intrinsic value is the difference between the option's strike price and the current market price; therefore, intrinsic value changes with the current market price, and is reflected in the premium. *Examples:* An investor owns an eBay April 65 put and the current market price of eBay is $58. The put has an intrinsic value of $7 (65–58). A General Electric June 30 call has intrinsic value when the market price is above $30 per share.

introducing broker A broker-dealer that does not hold cash or securities for its clients, such as a futures broker who has a working relationship with clients, but does not carry their accounts. Instead, it delegates, or introduces, the client accounts to a clearing broker-dealer, which may hold the client's cash and securities in street name.

inventory turnover ratio An efficiency ratio that measures the number of times a company's inventory is sold and replaced. The goal is to have a higher ratio; a low ratio indicates the company has additional inventory storage expenses. The formula is:

$$\frac{\text{cost of goods sold}}{\text{year-end inventory}} = \text{inventory turnover ratio}$$

inverted yield curve *See* yield curve.

investment adviser (*also called* an account executive, broker, investment executive, or stockbroker) An employee of an NASD or NYSE-member firm, who gives clients advice on which securities to buy and sell. An investment adviser may be paid in a number of ways: commission generated by buy and sell orders; a percentage of the value of a client's account; an hourly fee for the time spent working for the client; a fixed annual fee; or a combination of the above. An investment adviser has passed the Series 7 General Securities Representative Exam and the state law exam, and is registered with the SEC.

Investment Adviser Act of 1940 A federal law stating that a person who charges a fee for giving investment advice must register as an investment adviser. Exceptions are banks, attorneys, accountants, and noncompensated broker-dealers. Investment advisers must disclose any conflicts of interest, such as whether they personally own a security they are trying to sell to their customers.

investment banker Brokerage firms that are in the investment banking business and act as underwriters to bring new issues to market and sell them to investors. They may act as managing or participating underwriters in an offering. Most investment bankers also carry on retail business, where they act as broker-dealers in trading securities for individual client accounts. *See also* syndicate, underwriters.

investment company A company that pools money it receives from investors and invests in securities in accordance with specified objectives. Examples are open-end companies (mutual funds) and unit investment trusts (UITs). An investment company is owned by at least 100 investors; its securities are offered to the public, and it has a system of redeeming shares presented by investors. *See also* mutual fund, unit investment trust.

Investment Company Act of 1940 The federal law that gives the SEC authority to regulate investment companies.

investment grade Bonds rated BBB or higher by Standard & Poor's or Baa or higher by Moody's. *See also* bond rating.

investment objective The reason a client is investing. Brokers must ask the right questions to help clients explain their investment goals. Possible investment objectives are:

- *Diversification:* Concentration of investments in a single company or sector exposes clients to risk. Examples of clients who need to diversify are one who has retired from a company with most of her retirement plan invested in the company's stock, and one who believes he should invest only in pharmaceutical stocks.
- *Growth:* Increase in the value of an investment over a period of time, can be achieved by price appreciation, dividend reinvestment, or both. A typical client who might need growth is a younger investor who wants to save for retirement.
- *Income:* Comes from investments that pay dividends and interest, such as bonds, some stocks, and mutual funds. Someone older who needs monthly income is the kind of client who might have an objective of income.
- *Liquidity:* Some clients need to have immediate access to their money. A liquid investment is one that can be converted to cash quickly without loss of value.
- *Safety:* Preservation of capital is very important to many clients. They have worked hard to acquire their wealth and don't want to lose it in the stock market but want to earn more than they would with a savings account.
- *Speculation:* High-risk investments are called speculative. In exchange for taking the risk, clients invest for higher-than-average returns. Speculative investments may be appropriate for many clients, but only as a small percentage of their total portfolio.
- *Tax relief:* Many clients need ways to reduce their taxes. IRAs are one way to invest and let the account appreciate tax-free; taxes are paid only as funds are withdrawn from the account. Depending on the state where the investor lives, municipal bonds may be a good recommendation if their interest is free of federal tax.

See also suitability.

investment pyramid   A system of asset allocation that ranks investments according to safety: At the bottom are the safest investments, in the middle are growth investments with some risk, and at the top are the speculative investments. *See also* asset allocation, investment objective, risk.

High Risk
Speculative
bonds, stocks,
options

Moderate Risk
Small-cap and emerging growth
stocks; lower-investment-grade
bonds

Some Risk
Large-cap stocks; growth and income mutual
funds; investment grade bonds

Little or No Risk
Cash; U.S. Government securities; FDIC-issued CDs, savings
accounts, money market funds; AAA-rated bonds.

investor   A person or an organization that buys securities with the goal of earning income or making a profit.

IPO *See* initial public offering.

IRA (*also known as* individual retirement account)   IRAs were created by Congress to encourage people to save for their retirement. There are several types of IRAs: traditional IRAs, Roth IRAs, SIMPLE IRAs, and simplified employee pension plans (SEPs). IRAs may contain many types of investments, such as stocks, bonds, certificates of deposit, and mutual funds. Though option contracts are generally not allowed, some custodians allow covered call-writing. Collectibles, such as art, antiques, gems, or stamps, are not permissible, except for some U.S.-minted gold and silver coins. Anyone with earned income may contribute to an IRA, whether or not they are covered by a qualified corporate retirement plan. The contribution may or may not be tax deductible, depending on the saver's adjusted gross income and participation in a qualified plan. Traditional IRAs may be set up with a bank or brokerage firm. In 2005, the contribution limit for a traditional IRA is $4,000, or $4,500 for individuals age 50 and older. Distributions taken before age 59 1/2 from a traditional IRA are both taxable and subject to a ten percent penalty, unless the account owner is totally disabled or meets other IRS exceptions. Distributions after age 59 1/2 are considered ordinary income, and are taxed at the owner's tax rate. At age 70 1/2 IRA owners must start taking distributions based on life expectancy tables. Failure to take the required minimum distribution results in a 50 percent penalty tax on the amount not distributed. See also Roth IRA, SIMPLE IRA, simplified employee pension plan (SEP), spousal IRA.

IRA custodian A fiduciary, which may be a bank, brokerage firm, mutual fund or credit union, whose retirement plans have been approved by the IRS. The custodian must make sure the plan stays within IRS rules, and report required information, such as contributions, distributions, direct rollovers, and tax withholding. An IRA custodian may charge fees for this service, which vary from custodian to custodian.

IRA direct rollover A method of transferring assets from a qualified plan that helps the owner avoid tax withholding. *Example:* When X quits his job, he is entitled to his vested retirement benefits. If he goes to work at a firm that will accept his retirement benefit or chooses to move his distribution to a traditional IRA, he should request a direct rollover. A direct rollover is reported to the IRS, but is not taxable. Unlike a 60-day rollover, there is no withholding, and 100 percent of the amount rolled over goes to the new IRA custodian. Direct rollovers to Roth IRAs are not permitted, but an account owner can make a tax-free rollover to a traditional IRA and then make a taxable conversion to a Roth IRA.

IRA rollover *(also called a* 60-day rollover, personal rollover*).* If an employee leaving a company does not request a *direct rollover* of vested benefits to a new IRA, the employee will receive only 80 percent of the IRA assets, and 20 percent will be withheld, but the full amount will be reported to the IRS as the gross distribution. To avoid taxes, the gross distribution must be rolled over within 60 days, and the employee must make up the difference to replace the 20 percent withheld. *Example:* Joe retires from his job with $100,000 due to him from the company's retirement account. If he had asked for a direct rollover to a traditional IRA at ABC Brokerage Firm, ABC would receive the $100,000 from Joe's retirement plan, the employer would report the direct rollover to the IRS, and there would be no tax liability.

If he decided to do a personal or 60-day rollover, Joe would receive 80 percent, or $80,000. The remaining $20,000 (20 percent) would be withheld as tax, but the full $100,000 would be reported to the IRS. If Joe wants to avoid taxes, he must find an additional $20,000 and deposit $100,000 in the new IRA. The $20,000 is a double-edged sword: it is withheld as tax, but is also considered a taxable distribution and subject to taxes and a ten percent penalty if Joe is under age 59 1/2.

IRA transfer (*also called* a trustee-to-trustee transfer) Assets held in a IRA that are sent directly from one custodian to another at the request of the owner, such as transfer of an IRA from one custodial brokerage firm to a different firm through the ACAT System. Securities and cash in the account are never sent to the client. The transfer is tax-free.

Comparison of IRA Direct Rollover, Rollover, and Transfer

	Withholding	Tax Liability
Direct Rollover	none	none
Rollover	20%	on $ amount of distribution, plus penalties
Transfer	none	none

Island An ECN, part of the Instinet Group, that offers subscription services that give individual investors as well as market makers access to trading services and to Island's limit order book; popular with small investors because of its access to the NASDAQ market. *See also* electronic communications networks (ECNs), fourth market.

issued stock Stock of a corporation that has been sold to shareholders. Many companies retain the rest of their authorized stock, unissued stock, for
- issuing at a later date to generate cash,
- stock dividends,
- allocation to the employee stock purchase plan or stock options,
- exchange for outstanding convertible bonds or preferred stock,
- redemption of outstanding stock purchase warrants.

See also authorized stock, outstanding stock, treasury stock, unissued stock.

issuer Any entity that offers or intends to offer its securities for sale. An issuer can be a corporation, municipality, or state or federal government agency.

joint account An account with two or more owners, any of whom may buy or sell securities for the account. If funds are withdrawn, checks must be issued in the names of all owners of the account, unless the brokerage receives instructions to the contrary signed by all owners. If securities are sold, all owners must sign the endorsement. Owners of joint accounts may be either joint tenants in common (JTIC) or joint tenants with rights of survivorship (JTWROS).

joint tenants in common (JTIC) A joint account in which the percentage of ownership by each person has been specified when the account was opened. *Example:* John Jones and Alice Jones have a JTIC account. John's ownership interest is 40 percent; Alice's interest is 60 percent. If John dies, 40 percent of the value of the account will go to his heirs, if Alice dies, 60 percent of the value of the account will go to her heirs. While they are alive, checks must be made payable to both, unless they have signed written instructions to the contrary.

joint tenants with rights of survivorship (JTWROS) A joint account in which, on the death of one owner, the deceased's interest passes to the surviving tenants. *Example:* Bob Smith and Mary Smith have a JTWROS account. If Bob dies, his interest in the account goes to Mary, and vice versa. While they are alive, checks must be made payable to both, unless they have signed written instructions to the contrary. If the account has more than two joint tenants and one tenant dies, the surviving tenants have equal claims on the whole account and own it jointly.

jumbo CD Certificates of deposit of $100,000 or more. Jumbo CDs generally pay a higher interest rate than regular CDs.

junk bond Speculative bonds, those that Standard & Poor's rates BB or lower or Moody's rates Ba or lower. The yields are high to offset the risk. *See also* bond rating.

Keogh plan A type of self-employed retirement plan that may be set up if some-one has net earnings from the business for which the plan is established. If the self-employed business owner has employees, they must be included in the plan if they are 21 or older and have at least one year of service. There are two types of Keogh plans: for defined-benefit plans, the maximum contribution allowed for 2005 is the lesser of 100 percent of the participant's average compensation for the three consecutive years of highest compensation as an active participant, or $170,000. For defined-contribution plans, the maximum contribution allowed is the lesser of 100 percent of compensation or $42,000. A defined-contribution plan may be either a profit-sharing plan, where a percentage of the business's profits are contributed, or a money purchase plan, where a set dollar amount is contributed each year whether there is a profit or not. Distributions from a Keogh plan may not begin until the participant is 59 1/2 or disabled.

kiddie tax A nickname for the tax on investment income for a child who is under 14. The kiddie tax applies only to investment income such as dividends or inter-est, not to income from wages. For the 2005 tax year, the filing threshold for a child with investment income is $800. Investment income of $800-$1,600 is taxed at the child's tax rate. If the child's investment income is over $1,600 it is taxed at the parent's rate. *See also* Uniform Transfer to Minors Act.

Know Your Customer Rule NYSE Rule 405, which requires brokers to know the financial situation of their clients and make recommendations for suitable investments. The rule is important. The NYSE has disciplined many stockbro-kers violating Rule 405 because they "failed to use due diligence to learn the essential facts relative to a customer." Penalties range from censure to huge fines.

L *See* money supply.

ladder *See* bond ladder.

lagging indicator A factor that confirms trends in the business cycle that appears after a trend has begun. The Conference Board publishes the Index of Lagging Indicators monthly. The seven lagging indicators are: average duration of unemployment, change in CPI for services, commercial and industrial loans outstanding, ratio of consumer installment credit to personal income, change in labor cost per unit of output, ratio of manufacturing and trade inventories to sales, and average prime rate charged by banks. *See also* economic indicator.

last in, first out *See* LIFO.

last trade price The price of the most recent trade of a particular security. The SEC says that no short sales may be executed below or at the price of the last trade, unless the previous trade was at a price higher than the one before it. Rules pertaining to plus tick, minus tick, zero plus tick and zero minus tick are based on the last trade price.

leading indicator A factor that predicts trends in the business cycle, appearing before a trend begins. The Conference Board publishes the Index of Leading Indicators monthly. The ten leading indicators are: average work week of manufacturing workers, average weekly initial claims for unemployment insurance, new orders for consumer goods & materials, vendor performance–slowdown in deliveries, new orders for capital goods, building permits for private housing, Standard & Poor's 500 stock prices, M-2 money supply, interest rate spread on 10-year Treasury bonds, and consumer confidence. Positive changes in these factors indicate a period of growth ahead, negative changes indicate contraction. *See also* economic indicator.

LEAPS (Long-term Equity AnticiPation Securities) Equity or index options with a long term to expiration, up to three years. Equity LEAPS expire in January of each year, on the Saturday following the third Friday.

Index LEAPS are long-term options based on either one-tenth of the value of the underlying index or on its full value. *Example*: The ABC Index's value is 310, which represents an underlying value of $31,000 (310 x 100). The one-tenth value ABC Index LEAPS would be based on an index value of 31, with an underlying value of $3,100 (31 x 100). Index LEAPS are cash-settled based on the difference between the settlement value of the index on exercise date and the exercise price of the option. Index LEAPS may be either American or European-style. They may be sold in the open market before exercise. Index LEAPS expire in January and December of each year, on the Saturday following the third Friday.

legal opinion The opinion of bond counsel that must be attached to municipal bond certificates unless they are stamped "ex-legal". The legal opinion attests that the bond is tax-exempt and speaks to other legal questions that may impact bondholders. The bond counsel may issue either an unqualified legal opinion given without restriction or a qualified opinion indicating that bond counsel has reservations about the issue.

legislative risk The risk that changes to laws, especially tax laws, can affect investments. For example, Congress has written laws that virtually eliminate the strategy of postponing capital gains using a short-against-the-box strategy, and changed the law on passive income, affecting many owners of limited partnerships. *See also* risk.

letter of authorization (LOA) A letter to a brokerage firm signed by all account owners before any action is taken that would change the ownership of cash or securities in an account. An LOA is required, for example, when cash or securities are moved from one account to another, or funds withdrawn from a joint account are made payable to only one account owner or to a third party.

letter of intent (1) In securities underwritings, the agreement signed by the issuer and the underwriter. The underwriter agrees to buy the securities being issued and sets an approximate date of purchase and a price range. *See also* underwriting agreement.

(2) In mutual funds, a nonbinding agreement to invest a certain amount in a mutual fund over a 13-month period to allow shareholders to qualify for a reduced sales charge based on the amount invested. If at the end of the 13 months the shareholder has not invested the amount intended, the sales charge will be adjusted to the full amount. *See also* breakpoint.

level debt service *See* debt service.

leverage The use of borrowed capital by a company, such as proceeds from a bond offering, to increase earnings, or by individuals, using cash borrowed from margin accounts, to purchase securities with a minimum of cash. *See also* debt-to-equity ratio, margin account.

liability Amounts owed by a company to creditors, employees, and shareholders. *Current* liabilities are debts due within 12 months, such as accounts payable; accrued wages payable (hourly wages, salaries, and commissions); current long-term debt (any distributions of long-term debt payable within 12 months); taxes; and other short-term debt. *Long-term* liabilities are debts payable after 12 months, such as outstanding corporate bonds, loans, or promissory notes.

LIFO (last in, first out) A method of accounting that assumes that the last item purchased, whether inventory or shares of stock, is the first item sold. *See also* FIFO.

limited partnership A business owned by two or more individuals, one of whom is the general partner with full responsibility and the others of whom are passive investors with limited liability, that allows for flow-through of income, gains, losses, and tax benefits directly to the owners. The business itself pays no tax because the tax liability is apportioned among the investors. Limited partnerships invest in projects like oil and gas programs, real estate ventures, condominium development, or agricultural programs. Because of changes to the tax law on passive income, limited partnerships have lost appeal.

limited tax bond Municipal general obligation bonds issued by a taxing district that has limits on the amount of tax it can collect. For example, property taxes may be limited to a certain percentage of assessed valuation.

limited trading authorization (*also known as* trading authorization limited to purchases and sales of securities) Permission given to an appointee by the owner to make to make investment decisions for an account. Cash or securities may not be withdrawn from the account. *See also* discretionary account, full trading authorization.

limit order An order carrying a maximum or minimum buying or selling price. *Example:* A limit order to buy 100 shares of the Gap at $17.50 means that the client will not pay any more than $17.50 per share but may pay less if the price moves down. A limit order to sell 100 shares of the Gap at $17.25 means that the client will accept no less than $17.25 per share, but may receive more if the price moves up.

If the order cannot be filled at the limit price, the broker takes the order to the specialist, who enters the order in the specialist order book. If the price reaches the limit, the specialist may fill the client's order. However, not all limit orders are filled at the moment the price reaches the limit. A limit order entered in the book earlier may take precedence, which is called "stock ahead." Limit orders are accepted on all exchanges and over the counter.

liquidity (1) The ease of converting an asset to cash. High-volume NYSE stocks like GE and Xerox are said to be liquid because there are always buyers. A stock that trades on the Pink Sheets with volume of 500 shares a week is illiquid, because a seller would have a difficult time finding a buyer for 1,000 shares. Low-volume stocks are said to be "thinly traded."

(2) Working capital, the amount of money a company has to meet its short-term obligations. The formula for working capital is:

Current assets – Current liabilities = Working Capital

liquidity ratio (*also called the* current ratio) A measure of a company's ability to meet its short-term obligations. The working capital equation above measures the dollar amount of liquidity. The ratio can be used to compare one company's liquidity against another: The higher the ratio, the more liquid the company. The formula is:

$$\frac{\text{Current assets}}{\text{Current liabilities}} = \text{Liquidity ratio}$$

See also acid-test ratio.

liquidity risk The possibility that an investor may not be able to find a buyer for her investment if she needs to sell. Most exchange-listed stocks are considered liquid; they have high volume of shares trading on most days. Investments like limited partnerships that are difficult to sell are considered illiquid. *See also* risk.

listed option (*also called* standardized option) A put or call that trades on a national securities exchange, such as the NYSE. *See also* option.

listed security Any security (stock, bond, option, right, warrant) quoted for trading on an exchange like the NYSE or the AMEX. *See also* exchange.

LOA *See* letter of authorization.

load A sales charge on a mutual fund. The fund's underwriter is compensated by adding the sales charge to the net asset value (NAV) of the shares. The NASD prohibits sales charges in excess of 8.5 percent of the amount invested. A fund's sales charges must be clearly explained in the prospectus. A load added at the time of purchase is called a *front-end load*. Other funds are structured with a deferred, or *back-end load. See also* back-end load, front-end load, 12B-1 asset-based fees.

load fund A mutual fund that charges a sales charge.

loan consent agreement The part of the margin agreement that gives the brokerage firm permission to loan out customer securities held in margin accounts, in an amount equal to the debit balance, to other firms. *See also* customer protection rule, margin agreement.

LOI *See* letter of intent.

London Interbank Offered Rate (LIBOR) The rate of interest at which international banks dealing in Euros borrow funds from other banks. The rate, set daily, is a widely monitored indicator of international short-term interest rates.

long market value The current value of securities held in an account, based on the previous day's closing prices.

long position Owning a security, contract or commodity. The investor has title to the security or has a right to it. Margin accounts will show an entry called "market value long." *See also* short position.

long sale Sale of a security the investor actually owns and will deliver to the buyer or buyer's agent to close the transaction. *See also* short sale.

long straddle The purchase of a call and a put on the same stock that have the same strike price and expiration date, as in simultaneous purchase of Eastman Kodak Jan 15 calls and Jan 15 puts.

Long-Term Equity Anticipation Securities *See* LEAPS.

long-term capital gain The gain on sale for more than its purchase price of a capital asset, such as securities, real estate or tangible property, that has been held more than one year.

long-term capital loss The loss on sale for less than its purchase price of a capital asset, such as securities, real estate or tangible property, that has been held more than one year.

M1, M2, M3 *See* money supply.

maintenance call *See* margin maintenance call.

maintenance excess   The difference between the NASD/NYSE's 25 percent minimum margin and the equity in a client's margin account. *See also* margin.

maintenance requirement The minimum amount of equity required by the NYSE in a margin account. The maintenance requirement varies with different types of securities. *See also* margin.

making a market A broker-dealer who is buying or selling a particular stock for its own account as well as for its own customers or other broker-dealers.

Maloney Act of 1938 The amendment to the Securities Exchange Act of 1934 that established self-regulatory organizations (SROs) like the NASD, which regulate the over-the-counter market the same way the exchanges oversee their members.

management fee *See* underwriting spread.

managing underwriters *See* underwriter.

margin The purchase of securities on credit. Reg T of the Securities Exchange Act of 1934 gives the Federal Reserve Board authority to regulate margin purchases and allows brokerage firms to lend money to customers to buy securities. The Federal Reserve Board maintains a list of securities approved for buying on margin (*see* marginable security). The Fed, SROs like the NYSE and NASD, and individual brokerage firms all have different margin requirements (see below). Brokerage firm (house) requirements, which must be at least as strict as SRO requirements, vary from firm to firm and may be adjusted *without notice*. The house maintenance numbers shown in the chart are a representative sample.

Margin Requirements

Type of Security	Regulation T (Initial)	NYSE/NASD	House
Stocks $5 per share and over	50% of cost	25% of market value	35% of market value
U.S. government securities	Exempt security	1% to 6% of market value, depending on maturity date	6% of market value
Municipal bonds	Exempt security	Greater of 15% of market value or 7% of principal	Greater of 20% of market value or 10% of principal
Convertible bonds	50% of cost	25% of market value	35% of market value
Nonconvertible corporate bonds	Greater of 20% of market value or 7% of principal	Greater of 20% of market value or 7% of principal	Greater of 25% of market value or 10% principal
Stock short sales	150%	Greater of 30% of market value or $5 per share	

To open a margin account, clients must read and sign a margin agreement, making sure they understand the risk, suitability, and costs associated with margin accounts. The customer must make an initial deposit *(the minimum margin)* of $2,000 or 50 percent of the initial purchase price, whichever is more. Initial purchases under $2,000 do not qualify for margin trading and must be paid in full. Once the minimum margin has been met, if the value of the securities drops below $2,000, there is no maintenance call. In 2001 the SEC approved special margin rules for day traders: a pattern day trader, an investor who executes four or more day orders within five business days, has a minimum margin requirement of $25,000.

Example to explain margin accounting: A client buys 1,000 shares of Coca-Cola at $50, for a total investment of $50,000. The client must deposit 50 percent of the purchase price, or $25,000. The client's account is now:

Market Value Long	Debit Balance	Credit Balance	Client's Equity	Percent of Equity
$50,000	$25,000	0	$25,000	50%

Once the client meets the 50 percent deposit requirement, NYSE/NASD and house maintenance requirements take over. Reg T will no longer be an issue, unless the client makes another purchase or withdraws funds.

Equity is the market value of securities minus the amount *borrowed*. As the market value rises, so does the client's equity; as market value falls, so does the client's equity. The debit balance, or amount borrowed, remains the same until the client deposits cash to the account.

For example, if the price of the stock goes down to $40:

Market Value Long	Debit Balance	Credit Balance	Client's Equity	Percent of Equity
$40,000	$25,000	0	$15,000	37%

If the price of the stock goes up to $55:

Market Value Long	Debit Balance	Credit Balance	Client's Equity	Percent of Equity
$55,000	$25,000	0	$30,000	54%

An increase in the price of the stock (the market value) creates *excess equity* for the client, which may be used to purchase more stock or withdrawn as cash. To calculate excess equity:

$55,000	Market value long
-25,000	Debit balance
30,000	Equity
- 25,000	Reg T requirement
$5,000	Excess equity

With $5,000 in excess equity, the Reg T 50 percent requirement allows the client to buy $10,000 in securities *(buying power)*. Buying power is calculated by multiplying the excess equity by two (the reciprocal of 50 percent):

Reg T excess equity x 2 = buying power

Instead of buying more stock, the client may withdraw the $5,000 in excess equity in cash, which will result once again in a fully margined account at 50 percent equity.

Short sales executed in a client's margin account have other Reg T margin requirements. For short sales, Reg T requires that the account carry 150 percent of the current market value of the security, the first 100 percent coming from proceeds from the sale of the stock and the additional 50 percent from the investor. *Example:* A client shorts 500 shares of a $25 stock. The margin requirements would be:

Security sold short	Proceeds from the sale	Reg T (50%)	Cash required
500 XYZ Corp at $25.	12,500	$6,250	$18,750

The reason so much cash is required is the risk: if the price of the securities goes up, the risk is unlimited. The investor has to keep 150 percent of the stock's value in the margin account until she buys the stock to close the position. A client who opens a margin account with a short sale must deposit the NYSE/NASD $2,000 minimum, even if the Reg T requirement is less than $2,000.

Margin accounts are valued at the end of each business day. Recalculating the client's equity position is called *marking to the market*.

For more information: NASD: www.nasd.com/Investor/Trading/Margin/, SEC: www.sec.gov/investor/pubs/margin.htm.

margin account An account opened by a client who wants to borrow funds to purchase securities. The client signs a Margin Agreement form, which outlines the terms under which credit will be offered. The securities bought on margin are held as collateral for the loan. If the securities in the account decline in value, the investor may be required to deposit more cash to bring the value of the account up to the minimum requirement. Clients may also borrow money against the value of the securities in their margin account.

Clients who want to open margin accounts must meet minimum financial requirements. *See also* broker call rate, cash account, margin, margin agreement, margin maintenance call, Regulation T.

margin agreement The agreement signed by clients opening a margin account. The margin agreement has three parts: The *credit agreement* discloses the terms under which credit is offered. The *hypothecation agreement* gives the brokerage firm permission to use the securities in the margin account as collateral for a loan. The *loan consent agreement* gives the brokerage firm permission to lend securities held in the margin account to other firms. Clients must make sure they understand the risk, suitability, and costs associated with margin accounts.

margin call *See* margin maintenance call, Regulation T call.

margin department The part of a brokerage firm's back office responsible for handling clients' cash deposits to accounts, accounting for margin account balances, and notifying brokers of maintenance calls, past due notices, and extensions of credit.

margin maintenance call A demand that a client whose equity in a margin account has dropped below a brokerage firm's minimum maintenance requirement deposit more cash or securities or risk a forced sell-out. Reg T applies only to initial deposits; NYSE/NASD and house maintenance requirements take over after the initial purchase. Equity is the value of securities less the amount borrowed. The following chart illustrates how a drop in the market value of securities can lead to a margin maintenance call in an account with a 35 percent equity requirement. If the market value drops from $50,000 to $35,000, the percent of equity is at 28 percent ($10,000 ÷ $35,000 = 28%), and the account owner must deposit at least $2,250 to bring the account equity up to the required 35 percent, which is $12,250. Maintenance calls must be met promptly or the firm may sell some or all of the client's securities to cover the amount due.

Market Value of Securities	Amount Borrowed	Client's Equity	Percent of Equity	Required Equity (35%)
$50,000	$25,000	$25,000	50%	$17,500
$45,000	$25,000	$20,000	44%	$15,750
$40,000	$25,000	$15,000	37%	$14,000
$35,000	**$25,000**	**$10,000**	**28%**	**$12,250**

The client may satisfy the margin call by (1) depositing cash to reduce the debit balance, (2) selling some securities and using the proceeds to pay down the debit balance, or (3) depositing more marginable securities with a loan value equal to the amount of the call to increase the market value of the account. The loan value of stock is the complement of the minimum maintenance requirement: if that is 45 percent, the loan value would be 55 percent (100 - 45 = 55). Reg T for initial deposits is currently 50 percent, so the loan value is 50 percent. The client who has a maintenance call of $2,250 may deposit stock with a value of $4,500 to meet the call.

$$\frac{\text{Margin call in \$}}{100\% - \text{Reg T}} = \text{Reg T call} \quad or \quad \frac{\$2,250}{50\%} = \$4,500$$

Cash dividends from stock held in a margin account may be used to reduce any debit balance. Interest charged by the brokerage firm will increase the debit balance.

If the percentage of equity in a margin account falls between Reg T (50 percent) and the 25 percent maintenance requirement, the account becomes restricted. In restricted accounts, the client may not withdraw securities without depositing 50 percent of their value. *See also* restricted account.

margin of profit ratio (*also called* the operating profit ratio) A ratio that measures a company's profits in relation to its sales–its operating efficiency. The goal is a high ratio; a low ratio means operating costs are high, lowering profits. The formula is:

$$\frac{\text{Operating profit}}{\text{Net sales}} = \text{Margin of profit ratio}$$

See also net profit ratio.

margin risk The risk that the value of securities purchased on margin may decline, forcing the account owner to deposit additional cash or securities to avoid a forced sale, or that maintenance requirements may increase without notice. Though a brokerage firm may try to contact the client before selling securities to cover a margin call, it is not required to do so. Moreover, if there is a forced sale, the client may not be able to choose which security to sell. Brokerage firms are not obligated to offer extensions of time for clients to meet margin calls. Clients with margin accounts should pay close attention to the markets and the stocks held on margin. *See also* risk.

marginable security Securities identified by the Federal Reserve as eligible for purchase on margin. Marginable securities are stocks and bonds listed on a major U.S. stock exchange (NYSE, AMEX, and regional exchanges), NASDAQ National Market System (NMS) issues, and specified NASDAQ issues not included in the NMS but with enough trading volume to be included on the OTC Margin List.

Securities not eligible for margin are put and call options, over-the-counter stocks not approved by the Federal Reserve, and rights. New issues that might otherwise quality for the OTC Margin List, including public offering securities and mutual funds, are not marginable until 30 days after issue. After 30 days has expired, federal and house margin criteria and price stability determine whether the stock becomes marginable.

Exempt securities that do not fall under Reg T are U. S. Treasury bills, notes and bonds, government agency and municipal securities, and nonconvertible corporate bonds. These may be purchased on margin, and NYSE, NASD and house margin criteria determine loan value. *See also chart under* margin.

mark to the market The practice of checking the prices of securities held in margin accounts at the end of each trading day and comparing their value to the equity in the account. *See also* margin.

markdown *See* markup.

market A system in which securities are traded. Securities markets are thought of in terms of the *primary market* for new issues; the *exchange market*, such as the NYSE and the AMEX; the network of dealers called the *over-the-counter (OTC) market*; the *third market,* for listed stocks trading in large blocks on the OTC market; and the *fourth market*, also known as Instinet. *See also* exchange, fourth market, initial public offering, over-the-counter (OTC) market, third market.

marketability risk (*also called* liquidity risk) The risk that an investor may not be able to find a buyer for her investment if she needs to sell. Most exchange-listed stocks are considered highly marketable; large numbers of their shares trade on most days. Investments such as limited partnerships have much more marketability risk. *See also* risk.

market arbitrage Arbitrage that deals with differences in prices when securities trade on more than one exchange. *Example:* Barney's Building Materials trades on both the NYSE and the PCX. The best price on the NYSE is bid 23.125, ask 23.25. On the PCX, the best price is bid 23.75, ask 24. An arbitrageur would place simultaneous orders to buy at 23.25 on the NYSE and sell at 23.75 on the PCX, making a profit of 50 cents per share. *See also* arbitrage.

market efficiency theory *See* efficient market theory.

market maker A broker-dealer that buys or sells a particular stock for its own account. It stands ready to buy from or sell to its own customers or other broker-dealers. *See also* inside market.

market not-held orders *See* not-held (NH) orders.

market-on-close orders Orders executed at, or as close as possible to, the close of the day's trading. Market-on-close orders must reach the trader before the end of trading, or the order is canceled.

market order An order to buy or sell sent to the floor of an exchange without any restrictions. A market order to buy will be filled at the lowest current offering or asking price, a market order to sell at the highest current bid price. Market orders must be executed immediately.

market risk The risk of price volatility, a problem in both stock and bond markets, that may lead to loss of principal. The stock market, driven by investor emotions, tends to be more temperamental than the bond market. The bond market, however, is driven by interest rates, so that if interest rates go up, bond prices go down. An investor who sells a bond before maturity risks loss of principal if interest rates have risen since the bond was purchased. *See also* risk.

market value The current price of a security in the market in which it is traded, usually determined by investor supply and demand. *See also* book value, mark to the market.

markup The fee for services of a dealer acting as principal and buying and selling securities for his own accounts. The NASD has adopted a markup policy of no more than five percent as a reasonable charge for brokerage services. This five percent rule is meant to serve as a guide, but the percentage can be exceeded if the costs of a transaction justify it. The policy applies to all over-the-counter transactions, including stocks, bonds, government and municipal securities. It does not apply to mutual funds, variable annuities, or securities sold in public offerings.

maturity The date on which the principal amount of a bond is due to be paid to the investor, and the bond retired by the issuer. *See also* balloon maturity, serial maturity, term maturity.

mediation A method of resolving disputes among parties; an informal process where a neutral third party, a mediator, helps the two sides come to agreement. The mediator does not prescribe the solution but instead acts as a facilitator to help the parties work out a solution themselves. The NASD maintains a pool of mediators to hear cases. *See also* arbitration.

member A person who has trading privileges on a stock exchange. On the NYSE, a member may buy a seat on the exchange; pay a fee for physical access to the trading floor; or pay for electronic access, which does not include floor trading. The NYSE currently has 1,366 members.

member firm A brokerage firm with at least one employee or officer who is a member of a stock exchange. Stock exchange memberships are in names of individuals but their firms have all the benefits of membership.

member order The lowest priority for orders for new issues. Underwriting syndicates must establish the priority to be given to different types of orders and make them available in writing to all interested parties. Most priority provisions give presale orders top priority, followed by designated orders, and member orders. A member enters the order for its customer.

merger arbitrage *See* risk arbitrage.

mini-max offering A variation of a best efforts offering in which an investment banking firm, acting as agent, tries to sell as much of the new issue as possible. The issuer sets a minimum number of shares that the underwriter must sell. If the minimum is not met, the offering is cancelled and all investors' money is returned. If the minimum amount is met, additional shares may be sold, up to a maximum number or shares. This type of offering is used with limited partnerships. *See also* best effort.

minus tick An execution price below the previous sale. *Example:* in a sequence of trades at 37.50, 37.45, 37.50, and 37.55, 37.45 is the minus tick. SEC rules prohibit short sales on a minus tick. *See also* plus tick.

misrepresentation An untrue statement by a broker to a client about qualifications, services offered, fees charged, or investments sold—one of the most common complaints to the NASD from investors. Clients who suspect misrepresentation should contact the firm's branch manager or compliance department immediately. *See also* the NASD's *"Common Investor Problems and How to Avoid Them,"* at www.nasd.com/Investor/Protection/best_practices.asp.

modern portfolio theory A sophisticated investment theory that recommends a mix of investments that give the investor the highest possible return for a given amount of risk, rather than focusing on either fundamental or technical analysis, The risk of an individual stock is not viewed in isolation but in relation to how that stock's price fluctuates in relation to the value of the entire portfolio.

monetary policy Management by the Federal Reserve of the nation's money supply to meet its objectives for the size, movement, and growth of the economy. The Fed uses open market operations, the discount rate, and bank reserve requirements to influence the supply and demand for money. *See also* fiscal policy.

money market The market for short-term debt and securities, a source of funding for corporations, municipalities, and the U.S. government. Traded in the money market are bankers' acceptances, negotiable certificates of deposit, commercial paper, repurchase agreements, and Treasury bills. Maturities can be as short as overnight to up to one year. *See also* capital market.

money market fund A no-load, open-end mutual fund invested in short-term instruments. Though the NAV remains a constant $1 per share, interest rates may change as often as daily.

money supply All the money in the American economy. It is managed by the Federal Reserve Board. When there is too much money in circulation compared to the output of goods and services, interest rates are generally low and prices rise, which may lead to inflation; when not enough money is in circulation, interest rates are generally higher and prices drop, which may lead to recession. The Fed regulates the money supply by raising and lowering the discount rate, which is the interest rate that banks pay to borrow money from the Federal Reserve Bank. Economists divide money into four categories.

M1	M2
Paper currency and coins	M1, plus
Commercial bank checking accounts	Savings accounts
NOW accounts	Money market funds
Credit union share drafts	Overnight repos
Savings bank demand deposits	Overnight Eurodollar deposits
Nonbank traveler's checks	Time deposits under $10,000

M3	L
M2, plus	M3, plus
Time deposits over $10,000	Treasury bills
Repos held longer than one day	Savings bonds
	Commercial paper
	Bankers' acceptances
	Eurodollar holdings of U.S. residents

moral obligation bond A state-issued revenue bond; if revenues are not adequate to pay principal and interest to the bondholders, the state will meet the obligation through legislative appropriation, even though it is not legally required to do so.

moving average A method used by technical analysts to spot trends in the movement of the price of a stock or index. Most stock charts have sharp peaks and valleys that indicate prices; moving averages smooth out the jagged lines to display trends over a specified number of days. The two most popular types of moving averages are the simple moving average (SMA) and the exponential moving average (EMA). The most popular moving averages are the 20-, 30-, 50-, 100-, and 200-day averages. Shorter moving averages are more volatile, with more exaggerated results; longer ones, which move more slowly, give fewer indicators of change. Moving averages may be calculated using opening, high, low, or closing prices; the last are the most popular.

To calculate a 10-day SMA, add together the closing prices of the stock for 10 days and divide the total by 10:

$$8 + 9 + 10 + 9 + 10 + 11 + 10 + 11 + 12 + 13 = 103$$

$$103 \div 10 = 10.3$$

To keep the average *moving*, if the next day's closing price is 13, add the new price, 13, and drop the oldest price, 8:

$$9 + 10 + 9 + 10 + 11 + 10 + 11 + 12 + 13 + 13 = 108$$

$$108 \div 10 = 10.8$$

Then graph 10.3 and 10.8 and continue with the process, connecting the averages to form a smooth line. As each new day is added, the oldest is dropped and the average continues to move through time.

The disadvantage of an SMA is that it is a lagging indicator: it is always *behind* the price. If the price moves down, the SMA will remain above the price for a time, and it will be below the price when it moves. When trends change, moving averages can be deceptive.

To reduce the SMA lag, analysts use EMAs, which give more weight to the most recent price. The weighting used depends on the period the moving average covers. The shorter the period, the more weight is given to the most recent price; less weight is given to EMAs covering longer periods. EMAs react more quickly to changes in price than SMAs.

A number of web sites provide free stock charts with moving averages already calculated. For instance, www.stockcharts.com has a wide variety of chart options and a helpful tutorial.

MSRB *See* Municipal Securities Rulemaking Board.

municipal bond A long-term debt instrument that represents a loan by an investor to a state or local government, U.S. territory, or other public authority, such as an agency with jurisdiction over airports, ports, and bridges and turnpikes. Municipal bonds may have maturities of one month to over 50 years.

There are two types of municipal bonds: general obligation (GO) and revenue; the primary difference is the source of money to pay principal and interest to investors. Taxes generate the funds to replay GO bonds; for revenue bonds, the project's user fees are used to pay investors. The differences between the two types are summarized below.

General Obligation Bonds	Revenue Bonds
Backed by the full faith and credit of the issuer	Backed by the income-producing project
Used to fund capital projects that do not generate revenue, such as new schools, libraries, or city offices	Used to fund capital projects that generate revenue, such as utilities, airports, toll bridges
Financed by taxes	Financed by fees or income of the project
Require voter approval	Do not require voter approval
Competitive bidding process	Negotiated underwriting process
Rated	Not rated

The advantage of municipal bonds is that in most cases, interest is exempt from federal tax, though that depends on the issuer. Public purpose bonds are federally tax-exempt. Private purpose bonds may be taxable. Municipal bonds trade in the over-the-counter (OTC) market.

Municipal Securities Representative *See* Series 52 License.

Municipal Securities Rulemaking Board (MSRB) An agency created by Congress in 1975 to regulate the underwriting, trading, and sale of municipal securities, including bonds and notes issued by cities, counties, or states. The MSRB is an SRO subject to SEC rules.

municipal security *See* municipal bond.

Munifacts A subscription wire service of *The Bond Buyer* that provides information about proposed new municipal bond issues. *See also The Bond Buyer.*

mutual fund A registered investment trust company whose primary activity is investing. There are two types of mutual funds: open-end and closed-end. A mutual fund offers portfolios of different investment objectives, pools investors' money into the portfolio, and buys and sells securities based on cash flow in and out of the fund. Each portfolio is managed by an outside investment advisor or portfolio management company. Each investor owns an undivided interest in the portfolio, and shares in the gains, losses, and investment income of the portfolio. Sales of shares to customers are made at the public offering price (POP) and are redeemed at net asset value (NAV). The difference between the POP and the

NAV is the sales charge, or load, that the fund charges. The investment objective of a mutual fund must be clearly stated in its prospectus, and cannot be changed without a vote of the shareholders. Investment objectives are numerous, and include growth; income; growth and income; sectors, such as gold or technology; balanced, which may include income stocks and bonds; bonds; tax-exempt bonds; U.S. government securities; and money markets. Each prospectus is required to show a history of the fund's annual returns and state that past earnings are not an indicator of future performance. *See also* closed-end fund, load, no-load fund, open-end fund.

mutual fund switch The sale of one mutual fund and purchase of another in a different family of funds, for example, the sale of ABC Growth Fund and the purchase of XYZ Growth Fund. Clients who switch mutual funds may pay new sales charges, incur a capital gain tax liability, and lose some of the value of their investment by selling at NAV and buying at the POP. Though mutual fund switches are not recommended, they are sometimes justified. Compliance departments of brokerage firms may require clients to sign a statement that they understand the consequences of a switch. An alternative to a switch is an exchange, where the client's investment stays within the same family of funds, and new shares are purchased at NAV. *See also* exchange privilege.

mutual reciprocity (*also called* reciprocal immunity) Exemption of interest paid by municipal securities from federal income tax. The favorable tax status of municipal bonds means they can carry lower interest rates than taxable bonds, but to qualify for the exemption, the bonds must be issued to fund public projects. In some states, municipal bond interest may also be exempt from state tax.

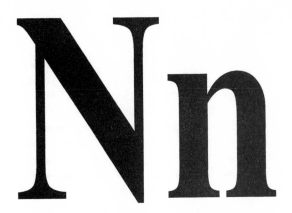

naked position *See* uncovered option.

NASD (National Association of Securities Dealers) The private-sector, not-for-profit SRO for the over-the-counter securities market. Under federal law, virtually every securities firm doing business with the U.S. public is a member of NASD. The NASD oversees 5,100 brokerage firms, over 99,000 branch offices and more than 660,000 registered securities representatives. The NASD registers member firms, writes rules to govern their behavior, examines them for compliance, and disciplines those that fail to comply. It also provides training for industry professionals and investors and is the largest securities dispute resolution forum, with arbitration and mediation programs, in the world. In 2000 the NASD began a restructuring plan which included sale of NASDAQ to the NASDAQ Stock Market. The NASD's web site is www.nasd.com. *See also* NASDAQ.

NASD Code of Arbitration Procedure The compilation of rules for resolving disputes between member firms, registered representatives, and the public. Any claim may be submitted for arbitration within six years of its occurrence. Monetary damages may be awarded to the claimant by the arbitration panel.

NASD Code of Procedure The compilation of rules for how NASD handles member violations of the Rules of Fair Practice. The Code of Procedure establishes the NASD's District Business Conduct Committees (DBCCs) to conduct disciplinary hearings.

NASD District Business Conduct Committee (DBCC) The local enforcement arm of NASD. DBCCs are composed of members of the securities industry elected to their positions by their peers to enforce compliance with the NASD by-laws and Rules of Fair Practice, federal securities laws, the rules of the Municipal Securities Rulemaking Board, and other securities regulations. Each of NASD's 11 Districts elects a DBCC.

NASD Manual A publication specifying NASD's role as an SRO. This publication contains all NASD rules under four headings:

- The Rules of Fair Practice define fair and ethical trade practices that must be followed by NASD member firms in dealing with the public. The NASD summarizes the rules as follows: promote just and equitable principles of trade for the protection of investors, prevent fraud and manipulative practices, consult with government and investors on matters of common concern, and prevent excessive commissions and charges.
- The Uniform Practice Code explains how member firms must do business with each other, including settlement procedures, rules of good delivery, ex-dates, confirmations, and don't know (DK) procedures.
- The Code of Procedure describes how the NASD handles member violations of the Rules of Fair Practice and sets up the District Business Conduct Committees to conduct disciplinary hearings.
- The Code of Arbitration Procedure governs resolution of disagreements between member firms, registered representatives, and the public, as well as monetary claims.

NASD Rules of Fair Practice *See* NASD Manual.

NASD Uniform Practice Code *See* NASD Manual.

NASDAQ The National Association of Securities Dealers Automated Quotation System, a computer system that gives brokers, traders, and market makers price quotations for over-the-counter as well as listed securities. NASDAQ provides three levels of stock quotations.

Level 1, for registered representatives, is available through public vendors and consists of real-time inside market bid/ask quotations (highest bid and lowest ask) for securities quoted in the NASDAQ system.

Level 2, for retail and institutional traders, consists of a full display of real-time quotations from individual market makers registered in every NASDAQ-listed security, as well as market makers' quotations on OTC Bulletin Board securities.

Level 3, for market makers, consists of Level 1 and Level 2 service plus the ability to enter quotations, execute orders, and send information. This service is restricted to NASD member firms that function as registered market makers in either NASDAQ, exchange-listed, or OTC Bulletin Board securities.

NASDAQ National Market *See* NASDAQ Stock Market.

NASDAQ SmallCap Market *See* NASDAQ Stock Market.

NASDAQ Stock Market A network of competing market maker firms linked by thousands of computers; it is not a stock exchange and has no physical location or address. Stocks of more than 5,000 companies trade on the NASDAQ Stock

Market, which is made up of two markets: the NASDAQ National Market, which lists more than 3,900 companies that are the larger and generally more actively-traded NASDAQ securities, and the NASDAQ SmallCap Market, which lists more than 1,300 smaller, less-capitalized companies. NASDAQ's total market capitalization was $2 trillion in 2002.

National Association of Securities Dealers *See* NASD.

National Association of Securities Dealers Automated Quotation System *See* NASDAQ.

NAV *See* net asset value (NAV).

negative yield curve *See* yield curve.

negotiability The transferability of a security. Common stocks are easily transferred: the owner of record signs the back of the certificate or a stock power and has the signature guaranteed by a brokerage firm or bank. Once this is done, the security is negotiable, or ready for transfer.

negotiated underwriting An underwriting in which an underwriter is appointed by the issuer after both have reached agreement on terms, such as the amount of securities to be offered, offer price, and fees. Negotiated underwritings are used most often for issues of corporate securities and municipal revenue bonds. *See also* underwriting agreement.

net asset value (NAV) The price per share based on a fund's total assets minus total liabilities, divided by the number of shares outstanding. NAV is comparable to a corporation's book value. The formula for calculating NAV is:

$$\frac{\text{Total assets } - \text{ Total liabilities}}{\text{Total shares outstanding}} = \text{NAV}$$

Example: A mutual fund has total assets of $100 million, total liabilities of $10 million, and five million shares outstanding. Its NAV would be $18:

$$\frac{\$100 \text{ million } - \$10 \text{ million}}{5 \text{ million}} = \$18$$

Mutual fund shares are bought and sold at NAV. Some funds add a sales charge, also called a load, to purchases. Net asset value plus a sales charge is called the public offering price (POP). Funds may also subtract a fee on redemption.

NAV is calculated once each business day, based on the previous day's purchases and redemptions.

net asset value per bond A measure of a firm's ability to meet its long-term debt obligations. NAV compared to the number of bonds outstanding shows the assets available to meet a company's obligations to creditors.

$$\frac{\text{Net assets - Current liabilities}}{\text{Number of bonds outstanding}} = \text{NAV per bond}$$

net profit ratio A measure of a company's operating efficiency, taking into consideration taxes and debt service. The higher the percentage of profit lost to taxes and interest, the lower the ratio. The formula is:

$$\frac{\text{Net income}}{\text{Net sales}} = \text{Net profit ratio}$$

See also margin of profit ratio.

net revenue pledge The promise by the issuer of a revenue bond to pay operating and maintenance expenses first, before debt service. *See also* gross revenue pledge, flow of funds.

new account form A form filled out and signed by broker and client, reviewed and approved by the branch manager, and filed at the brokerage firm whenever a new account is opened. The form contains information about each person who will have access to the account, such as name, mailing address, phone numbers, Social Security or tax identification number, occupation and employer, citizenship, basic financial information, investment objective, investment experience, and whether the client is an employee of another broker-dealer firm. If any information changes significantly, the new account form should be updated. *See also* Know Your Customer Rule.

new issue *See* initial public offering.

New Issues Act *See* Securities Act of 1933.

New York Stock Exchange (NYSE) (*also known as* The Big Board) A double-auction market that traces its roots to 1792 and was registered with the SEC in 1934 as a national securities exchange. The NYSE is home to approximately 2,800 U.S. and non-U.S. companies valued at nearly $20 trillion. Membership is required to buy and sell securities on the trading floor. A member firm is a company or individual who owns a seat on the trading floor; since 1953, the number of seats has remained constant at 1,366. In addition to being an exchange, the NYSE is one of the SROs recognized by the SEC. The NYSE is located at 11 Wall Street in New York City. Its web site, www.nyse.com, is an excellent source of information.

NH *See* not-held orders.

nine-bond rule An NYSE requirement that all bonds in quantities of fewer than ten be shown on the floor of the NYSE for at least one hour to ensure a fair chance for small investors to receive the most favorable price. Clients may request that their bond orders go straight to the over-the-counter market, where most bonds trade; if they do so, the broker-dealer must act as a broker, and not as principal.

no-load fund A mutual fund that sells its shares directly to investors without a sales charge, at NAV. Load is synonymous with sales charge or commission. No-load funds distribute shares to investors without going through an underwriter. The fund pays all sales expenses.

nominal owner *See* nominee.

nominal quote A quote between broker-dealers in the interdealer market that is used for inactive stocks; a market maker will give an indication of the price the stock would be if there were an active market for it. *See also* firm quote, subject quote, workout quote.

nominal yield *See* coupon yield.

nominee The name on an issuer's records of the brokerage firm or bank holding stock for an investor in street name. *See also* beneficial owner.

nonaccredited investor A person or institution that does not meet the definition of accredited investor that appears in the Securities Act of 1933 Rule 215 and who therefore is not eligible to make certain investments. *See* accredited investor.

noncumulative preferred stock Preferred stock on which unpaid dividends do not accrue if a corporation reduces or suspends payment of dividends. *See also* cumulative preferred stock.

nondiversified management company A company that does not meet the definition of diversified investment company under the Investment Act of 1940. Some country funds or sector funds choose to concentrate their investments in one specialty. *See also* diversified management company.

noneligible security *See* marginable security.

nonexempt security A security that is regulated by SEC registration requirements and Reg T. The term covers almost all stocks, convertible corporate bonds, mutual funds, and options. *See also* exempt security, registration by coordination, registration by notification, registration by qualification, margin.

nonmarketable security A security that cannot be transferred to another owner, and cannot be bought or sold on an exchange or over the counter. Examples are Series EE, HH, and I savings bonds, bought through Treasury Direct or a bank, and redeemable only by the purchaser or the beneficiary.

nonpassive income Income generated by activities in which a person participates directly, such as wages or portfolio income (dividends, interest, annuities, or capital gains). *See also* passive income.

nonqualified plan A retirement or other employee benefit plan set up by a corporation or individual that does not meet the requirements of the IRS under Internal Revenue Code §401(a), so that contributions to it are taxable. Approval of the plan by the IRS is not required, and the plan is exempt from ERISA rules. *See also* qualified plan.

nonsystematic risk The possibility that one stock or bond will move in a direction opposite to the market in general. Natural disasters such as fires or floods, strikes, accounting irregularities, or attempted takeovers may make a stock move in the opposite direction from others in the same industry. *See also* systematic risk.

no-par stock A stock issued with an arbitrary dollar value assigned to it, as most common stocks are. Par is virtually meaningless to investors, since demand determines the market value of a stock. A preferred stock with no par value states the annual dividend as a dollar amount rather than a percentage; a $5.00 no-par preferred stock would pay an annual dividend of $5.00 per share. *See also* par value.

normal yield curve *See* yield curve.

not-held (NH) orders Market orders for which the client has given the floor broker discretion as to time and price of the trade. Unlike market orders, which must be filled immediately, the broker may watch the market for the best time to execute the trade. The broker is not held responsible if the client does not get the best price.

not rated (NR) (*also called* non-rated) Bonds that have not been given a rating by Moody's, Standard & Poor's, or other services. This has neither positive nor negative implications; it is simply a disclosure.

NR *See* not rated.

NYSE *See* New York Stock Exchange.

odd lot Any quantity less than the standard unit of stock trading. On major stock exchanges, an odd lot is fewer than 100 shares. For bonds, *see* baby bonds. *See also* bunching orders, round lot.

odd-lot differential A charge added to the price of a stock in a trade on an odd lot; bid and offer/ask quotations are based on round lots. The commission fee may also be higher. Example: An investor sells 100 shares of XYZ Corporation for $80 per share. Another investor sells 50 shares for $79.875 per share. The odd-lot differential is $0.125 per share.

odd-lot theory A technical analysis theory that assumes that small investors have terrible timing. The underlying belief is that when odd-lot sales are up (small investors are selling), the market will go up and it is a good time to buy.

offer (*also called* asked price in the OTC market) The lowest price at which a dealer will sell a security. A quote is a dealer's current bid and offer on a security, such as Bid 56, Offered 56.125. *See also* bid.

	Bid	**Offer/Ask**
Quoting dealer	Buys	Sells
Customer	Sells	Buys

offering A stock or bond being made available to the public for the first time. *See also* initial public offering, underwriting.

offering price The price per share at which new issues are sold to the public. If a new issue is priced at $12 per share, that is the offering price. Mutual fund shares are also new issues; their offering price is the NAV plus any load (sales charge). If the NAV of a mutual fund is $15 per share and it has a 4.5 percent load, its offering price is $15.675 ($15 x 4.5% = .675). *See also* initial public offering.

official notice of sale (*also called* an invitation to bid) The method by which an issuer of bonds announces its intention to issue bonds and requests competitive bids. Investment bankers respond by preparing bids and forming underwriting syndicates. Official notices of sale, which are published in *The Bond Buyer,* identify the securities to be offered: the date, time and place of the sale; the name of the issuer; the type of security; bidding instructions; interest payment dates; dated date and first coupon payment date; maturity structure; call provisions; name of paying agent; name of bond counsel; and the amount of the good-faith deposit that must accompany the bid.

official statement A disclosure document for bond offerings that is similar to a corporate prospectus. The official statement outlines information of interest to a potential investor, such as the purpose of the issue, the source of funds for paying principal and interest, financial information about the issuer, economic information about the community, summary of covenants of the trust indenture, and creditworthiness of the issuer. Just as corporations issue preliminary prospectuses, bond issuers first issue a preliminary official statement, but this does not constitute an offer to sell; only the final prospectus or official statement may make that offer.

OID *See* original issue discount (OID).

open-end fund A type of mutual fund that continuously offers new shares to the public by prospectus and redeems shares presented by investors. Open-end mutual funds have several advantages: diversification, professional portfolio management, and guaranteed redemption. *See also* closed-end fund, mutual fund.

opening transaction The purchase or sale of an investment that adds to the net holdings in an account. An opening transaction to buy increases a client's long position; one to sell increases a client's short position. *See also* closing transaction.

open market operations The Federal Open Market Committee (FOMC) of the Federal Reserve sets a target level for the federal funds rate. If the Fed wants to expand the money supply, the FOMC purchases U.S. Treasury securities in the open market. This increases the money in the banking system, stimulates growth, and puts downward pressure on the federal funds rate. Sales of Treasury securities by the FOMC in the open market have the opposite effect, decreasing the availability of bank reserves and forcing interests rates higher. *See also* Federal Open Market Committee (FOMC).

open order *See* good-till-canceled order.

open outcry A method of trading securities in which buyers and sellers shout out their bids and offers and use hand signals to communicate.

operating profit ratio *See* margin of profit ratio.

option A contract between two investors that allows the purchaser of the contract the right to buy or sell shares of stock or another asset for a stated price by a stated time. There are two types of options: calls and puts. A call option is the *right to buy* a security; a put option is the *obligation to sell* a security. The purchaser of the option may exercise the option (use it to buy the underlying security); let the option expire; or sell the option to another investor before the expiration date. Equity options are those related to common stock. Options may be created on a number of underlying investments, such as indexes, foreign currencies, or Treasury bills, notes, or bonds. *See also* call, put.

option account An account supported by an option agreement and opened by an investor who wishes to trade options. The investor must first be given a copy of the disclosure document, *Characteristics and Risks of Standard Options,* published by Options Clearing House. Levels of approval for option accounts range from highly conservative to extremely risky. Information provided by the investor on the option agreement determines the level of trading that will be approved by the branch manager, who may be a registered options principal (ROP). Final approval will come from a senior ROP (SROP) or a compliance ROP (CROP). A margin account may also be required. *See also* option agreement.

option agreement The agreement required of investors who wish to trade options. The client must provide investment history, financial information, and investment objectives before an option account can be opened.

option contract *See* option.

Options Clearing Corporation (OCC) A company that creates equity options with different strike prices for option-eligible stocks. *Example:* If a stock is trading at $50, OCC may issue options with strike prices ranging from 35 to 70. If the stock price moves significantly, OCC will create new options closer to the new price. OCC standardizes the option market, sets expiration dates, and clears put and call transactions as well as options on stock indexes, foreign currencies, interest rates, and futures. OCC is owned by the five exchanges that trade options: AMEX, CBOE, International Securities Exchange, PCX, and PHLX.

order book official (OBO) An options exchange employee who keeps track of limit orders and trades for his own account as a market maker.

order period The time during which a syndicate manager allocates orders from other members of the syndicate, without considering time of submission. The order period, which may last hours or a few days, is determined by the manager. *See also* underwriting.

ordinary income Money earned as wages, salary, commissions, tips, jury fees, honoraria, or severance pay. Ordinary income also includes taxable fringe benefits, such as vacation and sick pay. It is neither investment income nor capital gains.

original issue discount (OID) A discount built into the price of some corporate and municipal bonds when they are issued, usually because the bond's coupon rate is not competitive with interest rates on similar securities. OID is the difference between the discounted issue price and the face value. Each year the investor must report a portion of the OID as interest income, whether or not the investor actually receives payment. For example, zero-coupon bonds are issued at a discount, but pay no interest until maturity, but the OID on them is taxable. There are some exceptions, such as tax-exempt OID securities and U.S. savings bonds. Each year's portion of the OID is reported to the investor by the issuer or brokerage firm on Form 1099-OID. If an OID bond is sold before maturity, its cost basis must be adjusted (accreted) to reflect the accrued OID, and the investor realizes a capital gain. OID bonds held until maturity have no capital gains.

OTC Bulletin Board An electronic quotation service for OTC securities that do not meet the NASDAQ listing requirements. Owned by NASDAQ, the OTC Bulletin Board provides quotes and market-makers for more than 3,600 securities, including penny stocks, foreign and domestic securities, and ADRs. Direct participation programs (DPPs) are also eligible for quotation on the OTC Bulletin Board, which shows indications of interest and previous-day trading activity. A direct competitor is Pink Sheets LLC. *See also* Pink Sheets.

OTC market *See* over-the-counter (OTC) market.

out-of-the-money An option that is not worth exercising because the current market price is below the strike price, for a call, or above it, for a put. *Example*: An investor would not exercise a General Electric June 30 call if the current price of GE is $25, because it would be cheaper to buy it at the market price. Similarly, an investor would not exercise an eBay April 65 put if the current price of eBay is $70, because the profit would be higher if she sold at market. *See also* at-the-money, in-the-money, option.

outstanding stock Stock of a corporation that has been sold or distributed and is in the hands of the shareholders. *See also* authorized stock, issued stock, treasury stock, unissued stock.

overlapping debt *See* coterminous debt.

over-the-counter (OTC) market A market made up of dealers, most often brokerage firms, who buy and sell securities from each other by computer or telephone. The OTC market is not an exchange and has no physical address. Because most of the securities traded in this market are not listed on an exchange, they are called "unlisted" securities, but some securities trade on both an exchange and over the counter. Most OTC stocks have symbols of four or more letters (e.g., Apple Computer, AAPL; Intel, INTC; and Microsoft, MSFT).

owners' equity *See* shareholders' equity.

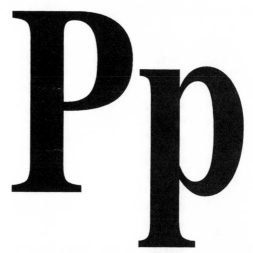

par A bond trading at a price equal to its face value; for example, a $1,000 bond purchased for $1,000 is said to be bought at par. *See also* discount, par value, premium.

par value (1) The face value or principal amount of a bond, usually $1,000; the amount of money the investor has loaned to the issuer. *See also* discount, premium.

(2) For a common stock, an arbitrary dollar amount given to the stock when it is first issued, often $1.00. It is virtually meaningless, since demand for the stock most often determines its market value. Many common stocks are now issued with no-par value. *See also* par, no par.

parity A method of awarding a trade on the exchanges when more than one order has the same bid or offer; the specialist awards the trade in the following sequence:

    1. Priority - first order received; if at the same time, then
    2. Precedence - largest order received; if the same size, then
    3. Parity - random drawing.
See also conversion parity.

participating preferred stock Stock that gives its holders the right to receive a portion of the company's profits in addition to their regular dividends. The company must first pay interest to bondholders, and dividends to other preferred stockholders and common stockholders. If there are any profits left over, participating preferred stockholders may receive additional dividends, up to an amount stated in the description of the stock. An example of participating preferred stock is ABC Corp. 5% Preferred Participating to 8%. ABC Corp. would pay an additional three percent dividend to holders of the participating preferred stock if there were enough profits. *See also* preferred stock.

partnership account A type of business account consisting of an unincorporated group of two or more people. Clients who wish to open partnership accounts must prove that the business has the legal right to own investments, give the names of people authorized to trade in the account, and state any limitations to the type of investment allowed. If a margin account is requested, the partnership must provide copies of a resolution authorizing it. If one partner dies, the partnership ceases to exist, all open orders must be cancelled, and the account must be frozen until proper documentation is provided by an administrator of the deceased partner's estate.

passive income Income generated by passive activity, which the IRS defines as "any activity involving the conduct of any trade or business in which you do not materially participate," such as a limited partnership. Passive losses may be used only to offset passive gains. *See also* nonpassive income.

pass-through security A mortgage-backed security created when bankers form a pool, or group of mortgages, sell interests in them, and pass through interest and principal payments from homeowners to the holders of the security. The most common pass-through securities are CMOs, REITS, REMICs, and those issued by FHLMC and GNMA.

pattern day trader An investor who executes four or more day trades in five business days, provided the number of day trades is more than six percent of the total trades in the account during that period. The SEC has set new margin rules for pattern day traders, one of which sets the minimum margin equity requirement at $25,000.

Patriot Bond Series EE savings bonds issued in response to Americans' desire to help support antiterrorism efforts. Money invested in Patriot Bonds is not earmarked for the war on terrorism but is deposited in the U.S. Treasury's general fund. Patriot bonds earn 90 percent of market yields on five-year Treasury securities with interest compounded semiannually. Patriot Bonds are redeemable any time after one year, but bonds cashed before five years are subject to a three-month interest penalty. Patriot Bonds stop earning interest at 30 years.

payable date The date on which shareholders will receive the dividend from the paying agent for a corporation. For an explanation of the relationships among the various dates related to dividends, *see* ex-dividend date.

paying agent The agent, usually a bank, responsible for distributing dividends to stockholders and principal and interest payments to bondholders.

payment date *See* payable date.

payroll deduction plan A retirement plan that allows employees to have money deducted from their pay and deposited directly into a qualified or nonqualified plan.

peak (*also known as* prosperity) The end of a period of expansion in the business cycle and the beginning of a contraction. *See also* business cycle.

pegging Stabilization of the price of a security, currency, or commodity by buying or selling to offset price fluctuations. In securities markets, the SEC allows pegging only for new issues; the managing underwriter is authorized to buy shares in the open market to stabilize the new issue. A country's central bank may also stabilize the exchange rate of its currency in relation to others by buying and selling it in the open market.

penny stock An OTC security that does not meet NASDAQ listing requirements; since most are priced at less than one dollar, they are called "penny stocks." Up to 1990 the penny stock market was unregulated. Companies issuing penny stocks were not required to report fully to the SEC, and individuals who had been banned from regulated markets operated freely in the penny stock market, which was filled with fraud and corruption. The Penny Stock Reform Act of 1990 was enacted to create a healthy primary and secondary market for penny stocks, which would protect investors and issuers alike. The SEC forbids broker-dealers to solicit penny stock orders, but customers may enter unsolicited orders. *See also* Pink Sheets.

P/E ratio *See* price/earnings ratio.

person "A natural person or a company," according to the SEC.

Pink Sheets An electronic and print quotation service for OTC securities that do not meet NASDAQ listing requirements. It lists recent bid and ask prices for each brokerage firm that makes a market in those securities. The names comes from the color of the paper they are printed on. Pink Sheets LLC is a direct competitor of NASDAQ's OTC Bulletin board. As of January 2003 there were 3,300 stocks listed on the Pink Sheets, which can be accessed at www.pinksheets.com. *See also* OTC bulletin board, Yellow Sheets.

placement ratio The percentage of the previous week's new municipal bond issues that were purchased from underwriters, published once a week by *The Bond Buyer.*

plus tick A price that is higher than the previous execution; for example, a stock that trades at 45 and the next time at 45.125. Plus ticks carry over from one day's close to the next day's opening session. Orders to sell short may be executed only on a plus tick or zero plus tick. *See also* minus tick, zero plus tick, short sale.

point The measure of bond prices; one point is equal to one percent of face value ($1,000). If the price of a bond goes from par (100) to 98, the bond has dropped two points, or $20. *See also* basis point.

political risk The possibility of civil unrest or unstable governments in third-world or developing countries that may affect the viability of an emerging market investments. *See also* risk.

POP *See* public offering price (POP).

portfolio An investor's combined holdings of assets.

portfolio income Income from the full range of an investor's holdings, including dividends, interest, annuities, and capital gains from the sale of securities. Portfolio income is nonpassive income.

portfolio theory *See* modern portfolio theory.

positive yield curve *See* yield curve.

power of substitution *See* stock power.

precedence A method of awarding a trade on an exchange if more than one order is received with the same bid or offer; the sequence the specialist follows is:

    1. Priority—first order received; if at the same time, then
    2 Precedence—largest order received; if the same size, then
    3. Parity—random drawing.

preemptive right A right offered by many companies that allows current stockholders to buy shares of additional common stock or securities that are convertible to common stock before any public offering. Preemptive rights allow shareholders to retain the same percentage of ownership in a corporation when new shares are issued. Preemptive rights particularly benefit large shareholders. *See also* dilution, rights.

preferred stock An equity security that works like a fixed income security. Preferred stock has a fixed dividend and interest rates affect its market price. Preferred stockholders must be paid dividends before common stockholders. They usually have no voting rights, but if the company is liquidated, their claim against the company's assets has priority over common stockholders. *See also* adjustable rate preferred stock, callable preferred stock, combination preferred stock, convertible preferred stock, cumulative preferred stock, participating preferred stock, prior preferred stock.

preferred stock ratio A measure of the safety of a corporation's bonds that looks at the percentage of total capitalization that is in preferred stock. The formula is:

$$\frac{\text{Preferred stock}}{\text{Total capitalization}} = \text{Preferred stock ratio}$$

preliminary official statement *See* official statement.

preliminary prospectus (*also called* a red herring) A prospectus provided to potential investors during the period when the SEC is reviewing a company's registration statement. It must carry a statement printed in red ink on the cover that a registration statement has been filed but is not yet effective. Because it does not contain final pricing information, potential investors must also be given the final prospectus after the SEC approves it. *See also* cooling-off period, prospectus.

premium (1) The amount by which a bond is priced above par. *Example*: A $1,000 bond has a current market price of $1,020. (2) The price an option buyer pays to the option writer. *Example*: A General Electric June 30 call has a premium of $1.65. Because each option contract covers 100 shares of stock, the premium is multiplied by 100, so the contract would cost $165. *See also* discount, par.

prepayment The request of a seller for the proceeds of the sale of a security before the settlement date. NYSE rules generally prohibit prepayments, but some brokerage firms may allow them in case of emergency. In those cases, the firm lends the money to the client and may charge interest. Prepayment requests must be approved by the firm's home office.

prerefunding Retirement of a series of bonds by replacing it with another series at a lower interest rate. Before the first call date of the original bonds, the issuer sells the new bonds and the proceeds are placed in an escrow account and invested in U.S. government securities with the interest being used to pay the interest on the first series of bonds. On the first call date, the prerefunded bonds are retired, with the escrowed funds used to pay back the investors. *Example:* The State of California had an issue of 5.625 percent bonds outstanding but interest rates prevailing in the market are lower than 5.625 percent. The first call date was May 1, 2004, and the state decided to retire the whole issue. California therefore issued a new series of bonds at four percent and put the proceeds in an escrow account to earn interest until May 1, 2004, at which time the entire 5.625 percent series was retired and the investors paid.

Prerefunded Bonds	New Bonds
State of California	State of California
5.625% due 5/1/10	4.00% due 5/1/15
Call 5/1/04	

Prerefunded bonds are considered extremely safe given the quality of the invested funds in the escrow account.

presale order Orders entered prior to the order period for new issues, which are given the highest priority. Underwriting syndicates must establish the priority to be given to different types of orders and inform all interested parties of them in writing. Most priority provisions give presale orders top priority, followed by designated orders, and member orders. No members are credited with takedown on presale orders. The entire spread, less the management fee, is credited to all the members of the syndicate according to their participation. *See also* underwriting spread.

present value The estimate of the worth of an amount of money today that will appreciate to a future value at a certain date. *Example:* A zero-coupon bond matures at $1,000 in one year. If the interest rate is four percent, the price would be $1,000 ÷ 1.04, or $961.54, the bond's present value.

price/earnings (P/E) ratio The comparison of a company's earnings to its stock price. If companies are in the same sector, the one with the higher P/E ratio is generally more expensive. Growth stocks usually have higher P/E ratios, because many investors are willing to pay a higher price for stable long-term growth. Cyclical stocks usually sell at lower P/E ratios, because their prices are subject to more fluctuation. Speculative stocks may have either high P/E ratios, because they are expensive, or low P/E ratios because they have little or no earnings. The formula for P/E ratio is:

$$\frac{\text{Current market price of common stock}}{\text{Earnings per share}} = \text{P/E ratio}$$

price spread *(also called a* vertical spread*)* The purchase of one option and the sale of another option in the same class (calls or puts on the same underlying security) that has the same characteristics except for the strike price. *Example:* An investor buys ABC Mar 25 calls and sells ABC Mar 30 calls. *See also* spread.

primary earnings per share *See* earnings per share (EPS).

primary offering A stock offering in which the proceeds of the underwriting go directly to the issuer. The offered shares can be new or additional issues. *See also* secondary offering, split offering.

prime paper Commercial paper that is highly rated by Moody's, Standard & Poor's, and other rating services. *See also* commercial paper.

prime rate The interest rate that banks charge their best customers, such as large corporations, for unsecured loans. Large banks set the prime rate, which is usually followed by smaller banks.

principal A person who buys or sells securities for his own account and charges a markup for this service. A brokerage firm may act as principal, buying securities from or selling securities to its clients. *See also* agent.

principal transaction The purchase or sale of a security by a broker-dealer acting as dealer in buying for its own account or selling from its own inventory. In principal trades, the broker is paid markup or markdown. *See also* agency transaction.

prior preferred stock *(also known as* preferred Class A) Stock with priority over other preferred stock in payment of dividends or distribution of assets if the company is liquidated. *See also* preferred stock.

priority A method of awarding bids or offers on an exchange when they are the same; the specialist awards the trade in the following sequence:

1. Priority: first order received; if at the same time, then
2. Precedence: largest order received; if the same size, then
3. Parity: random drawing.

private letter ruling An opinion issued by the IRS in response to a question about interpretation of tax law. Accounting firms, banks, brokerage firms, and other financial institutions often seek and receive private letter rulings.

private placement Stocks, bonds, and other investments sold to large private or institutional investors without a public offering. Private placements are generally exempt from the registration requirements of the Securities Act of 1933. *See also* accredited investors, Regulation D, private limited partnership.

Private Securities Litigation Reform Act of 1995 A federal law that eliminates frivolous investor lawsuits; creates a safe harbor for companies making good-faith forecasts of earnings and company growth; establishes rules for class-action lawsuits on plaintiff qualifications, terms of settlement, and attorney fees; sets uniform pleading standards; imposes mandatory sanctions for violation of Rule 11 of the Federal Rules of Civil Procedure; provides for proportionate liability of defendants; and sets requirements for outside auditors who discover illegal activity in the course of an audit.

proceeds transaction Use of the proceeds from the sale of one security to buy another at approximately the same time. The NASD five percent markup policy limits the combined commission and markup to no more than five percent of the purchase amount.

profit and loss statement *See* income statement.

profit-sharing plan A plan in which a percentage of a company's profits are set aside for employees to share. Annual contributions are made into an account for each employee. The funds in the account grow tax-free until withdrawal and may be invested in stocks, bonds, or mutual funds. *See also* Keogh plan.

profitability ratio Measures used to compare one company's profitability with that of its competitors in terms of profits in relation to sales. Common ratios are margin of profit ratio and net profit ratio. *See also* margin of profit ratio, net profit ratio.

program trade As defined by the NYSE, a basket of 15 or more stocks from the Standard & Poor's 500 Index or a basket of stocks from the Standard & Poor's 500 Index valued at $1 million or more.

program trading Trading entered into automatically when price ceilings and floors for stocks set by brokerage firms, institutional investors, and mutual fund managers are reached. At that point computers connected directly to the trading floor automatically place orders to buy or sell huge blocks of stocks. Program trading has been blamed for the rapid crash of 1987. Since 1989, circuit breakers have been used to solve the problem. *See also* circuit breaker.

progressive tax A taxing regimen, such as the federal income tax rates, where higher-income people pay a higher rate and therefore a larger share of taxes than those with lower incomes. *See also* regressive tax.

property dividend A dividend paid to shareholders in the form of stock in a subsidiary of the parent company or with products made by the company.

prospectus A document containing specific information about a stock or bond that is required by SEC rules, including information about the company's business, management, accounting firm, and legal opinions. The Securities Act of 1933 requires that all nonexempt public offerings of securities be sold by prospectus. No sales are allowed unless the investor has received a prospectus.

When the SEC clears a security for sale, it does not give its approval to the security; nor does it guarantee the accuracy of the disclosures of the company. It simply states that the company has submitted the required documentation:

> The Securities and Exchange Commission has not approved or disapproved of these securities. Further, it has not determined that this prospectus is accurate or complete. Any representation to the contrary is a criminal offense.

Mutual funds are sold by prospectus because each investor is buying newly issued shares with each purchase. Mutual fund prospectuses contain information about investment objectives, past fund performance, risk, fees and expenses, and sales charges. *See also* preliminary prospectus, official statement.

Prospectus Act *See* Securities Act of 1933.

proxy A method of shareholder voting in which the voters give to an assignee the right to vote their shares according to the shareholder's instructions. Broker-dealers holding shares in street name must forward proxy information to the clients who own the stock. Clients may forward their proxy vote directly to the corporation or give instructions to the broker-dealer. If the client does not respond, the broker-dealer may vote the client's shares if the motion is routine, such as ratification of the corporation's independent auditor; if the question is crucial, such as a merger or acquiring more debt, or involves a proxy fight, the broker-dealer may not.

proxy fight (*also known as a* proxy contest) A duel to attract shareholder votes in the case of a takeover attempt by another corporation or group of shareholders, usually in the context of an attempt to vote out company management. All participants in proxy fights, including anyone who gives advice to shareholders, must register with the SEC or face criminal prosecution. Brokers who simply answer shareholders' questions are not considered participants.

prudent man rule A standard by which fiduciaries, trustees, or custodians for others must act in making investment decisions for others. Their choices must be made with careful consideration to preserve capital and limit risk.

public offering price (POP) (1) The price at which new issues of stock or bonds in an initial or secondary offering are sold to investors. (2) The price of a mutual fund share, consisting of NAV plus a sales charge. It is the price per share based on the fund's total assets minus total liabilities, divided by the number of shares outstanding. The formula for calculating POP is:

$$\frac{\text{Total assets - Total liabilities}}{\text{Total shares outstanding}} = \text{NAV}$$

NAV + sales charge = POP

public purpose bond Any municipal bond issued to fund a project that benefits the general public, such as a bridge or hospital. A bond must be for a public purpose if its interest is to qualify as tax-exempt.

Public Utility Holding Company Act of 1935 A federal law regulating interstate holding companies in the gas or electric utility business. It requires those companies to submit periodic reports to the SEC on the organization, financial structure, and operations of the company and its subsidiaries. SEC approval is required for all mergers and acquisitions, securities offerings, and financing transactions.

purchase and sales (P&S) department The back-office department that handles the billing for buy and sell orders, generating trade confirmations. P&S is also the brokerage firm's liaison to the clearing corporation.

purchasing power risk *See* inflation risk.

put An option that gives the right to sell the underlying security at a predetermined price for a certain period of time. *Example:* The Intel March $30 put is a contract to sell 100 shares of Intel at $30 before the expiration date in March. *See also* put buyer, put writer, option.

put bond *(also called* tender option bond*)* A bond issued with an option for the bondholder to require the issuer to take back the bond at full face value before maturity date. Some puttable bonds have specific dates or a window of time when the put feature can be exercised; others can be exercised at any time. The put features allows the issuer to pay lower interest rates on these bonds.

put buyer An investor who pays a premium for an option contract that gives the right to sell the underlying security at a predetermined price for a set period of time. A put buyer is bearish on the underlying stock. *Example:* Believing that JKL is overpriced at $30 per share, an investor buys a JKL January $25 put, which gives her the right to sell 100 shares of JKL common stock at $25 before the expiration date in January. In November the price of JKL drops to $25 and continues to fall to $21. The investor buys 100 shares of JKL stock at its market price of $21 per share and then exercises her put to sell the stock at $25, for a profit of $4 per share. Also, instead of exercising the option, the investor could have sold her put option to another investor for a profit, because as the price of JKL common stock falls, the premium on the put increases. A put buyer's maximum potential gain is the strike price of the option less the premium. If the price of the stock had gone up, or if the put buyer had not exercised the option, it would expire worthless. The put buyer's loss is limited to the cost of the premium. *See also* put.

put spread The simultaneous purchase and sale of puts on the same security that have different strike prices, expiration dates, or both. Bearish investors buy the put with the higher strike price and sell the put with the lower strike price. The put with the higher strike price will have the higher premium, so the spread creates a debit in the client's account—a debit put spread. An example of a debit put spread is:

Buy ABC July 30 put for	5.50 (debit)
Sell ABC July 25 put for	<u>1.65</u> (credit)
	3.85 net debit

Bullish investors create put spreads by buying the put with the lower strike price and selling the put with the higher strike price. Because the put with the lower strike price will have a lower premium, the spread creates a credit in the client's account—a credit put spread. An example of a credit put spread is:

Buy XYZ Oct 30 put for	5.50 (debit)
Sell XYZ Oct 35 put for	<u>10.80</u> (credit)
	5.30 net credit

put writer The seller of a put; an investor who for a premium accepts the obligation to sell the underlying security at the predetermined price for a set period of time and at the discretion of the put buyer. *Example*: An investor who is bullish on eBay sells eBay April 65 puts. Put writers hope that the price of the underlying stock will remain the same or go up. If that happens, the put owner will not exercise the option, and the put writer keeps the premium, which is the maximum gain on the sale of a put. If the price of the stock drops and the put owner exercises the option, the put writer must buy the stock at the strike price. There is significant risk to writing puts: the difference between the strike price and zero, the lowest the stock price could go. In the eBay example, if the price were to go to 60, the owner of the put would exercise, and the put writer would be obligated to buy eBay at the strike price, 65.

qualified legal opinion An opinion on a bond issue indicating that bond counsel has reservations about the issue or wants investors to know that certain conditions exist, such as a pending lawsuit to block the project which the bonds are funding. *See also* unqualified legal opinion.

qualified plan A retirement plan set up by a corporation or individual that meets IRS requirements for tax deductibility, primarily that it be in writing, permanent, for the exclusive benefit of employees and their beneficiaries, and not discriminatory in favor of any group of highly paid employees. Private sector plans fall under the rules of the 1974 ERISA, which was passed to protect the rights of participants of qualified plans. *See also* nonqualified plan.

qualitative analysis A study that deals with intangibles–factors that cannot be measured in numbers. Municipal bond issuers use qualitative analysis to determine trends in population and property values, recent projects of a similar nature, and the fiscal inclinations of residents. For example, a fire district wanting to build a new fire station must take into consideration the growth of the area, the length of time since the last fire station was built, and the willingness of the residents to approve higher taxes to fund a bond issue for the station.

quantitative analysis A study that deals with tangibles–things that can be counted. Municipal bond issuers use quantitative analysis to determine population, the number of taxable properties in a municipality, or the number of users a project might have. For example, a fire district may have a population of 30,000, 9,000 homes and apartments, and 600 businesses; the estimated total assessed value of property in the district is $8.5 million. These numbers would be taken into consideration by the municipality in deciding whether to issue bonds to fund construction of and equipment for a new fire station.

quick ratio *See* acid-test ratio.

quiet period A period beginning when an issuer hires an underwriter for a security offering and ending approximately 25 days after the new security begins trading. During this time the issuer and its brokerage firms are prohibited from public comment or distributing materials other than preliminary or final prospectuses. Brokerage firms are not allowed to send out research reports during the quiet period.

quote The highest bid to buy and the lowest offer to sell at any given time. *See also* backing away, bid price, firm quote, nominal quote, offer, subject quote, workable indication, workout quote.

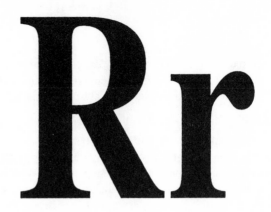

RAN *See* revenue anticipation note.

random walk theory The theory that the movement or direction of stock prices in the past cannot be used to predict their movement or direction in the future, based on the belief that stock prices are random and unpredictable.

ratings *See* bond rating.

real estate investment trust *See* REIT.

real estate mortgage investment conduit *See* REMIC.

realized gain The amount of profit an investor has on an asset that has been sold.

reallowance *See* underwriting spread.

recession A slowing of economic activity, marked by two or more quarters of a shrinking economy. GDP is the standard measure of American economic activity.

reciprocal immunity *See* mutual reciprocity.

record date The date on which a corporation determines who is and who is not eligible to receive an announced dividend. Owners of record on that date will receive the dividend. Corporations are required to announce dividends and notify the NASD and other SROs at least ten days before the record date. *See also* ex-dividend date.

recovery The part of the business cycle when the economy begins to rebound after a recession or depression. Characteristics of a recovery are growth in GDP, increased employment, improved customer confidence, and rising stock prices and interest rates.

redeemable security Shares issued by mutual funds and UITs. Investors who want to sell their shares sell them back to the fund or UIT at NAV.

redemption 1) Repayment of bond principal to an investor. Bonds may be redeemed on their maturity date or by being called before maturity. (2) The sale of mutual fund shares. When a mutual fund share has been sold, it is destroyed. Buyers of mutual funds always receive newly issued shares.

red herring *See* preliminary prospectus.

reducing orders Orders in the specialist's order book that are reduced in price because the stock goes ex-dividend; specifically, orders entered below the market, such as buy limit, sell stop, and sell stop limit. The price of the stock drops by the amount of the dividend, and prices in the specialist's book are adjusted, unless the client enters a do not reduce (DNR) order. *See also* do not reduce order.

refunding Retirement of a bond issue and its replacement with another series of bonds, often at a lower interest rate. *Example:* An issuer that has a series of eight percent bonds outstanding can issue six percent bonds and pay back the eight percent bondholders with the proceeds of the new issue. *See also* prerefunding.

registered as to principal only *See* registered bond.

registered bond A bond for which the name and address of the owner are recorded by issuer. *Fully registered bonds* have the owner's information on file with the transfer agent and on the face of the certificate and the interest payments are automatically mailed to the bondholder on each payment date. *Bonds registered as to principal* only have the owner's information on file with the transfer agent and on the face of the certificate, but interest coupons are attached. The bondholder must deliver the coupons to the paying agent to get the interest. *See also* bearer bond, book entry bond.

registered representative (*also called* account executive, broker, investment executive, stockbroker) An employee of an NASD or NYSE member firm who advises clients on which securities to buy and sell. A registered representative may be paid in a number of ways: commission generated by buy and sell orders, a percentage of the value of a client's account, an hourly fee for time spent working for the client, a fixed annual fee, or a combination of the above. A registered representative has passed the Series 7 General Securities Representative Exam and a state law exam and is registered with the SEC.

registered traders Members of an exchange who buy and sell mainly for their own accounts.

registrar A bank or trust company or other agent appointed by the issuer to keep track of the corporation's authorized stock, making sure that no more shares are issued than are allowed, and to certify that bonds issued by the company are legal.

registration by coordination A method of registering securities simultaneously at the state and federal levels, one of three ways provided by the Uniform

Securities Act to register securities. Nonexempt securities must be registered in each state in which they will be sold. *See also* registration by notification, registration by qualification.

registration by notification (*also called* registration by filing) A method of registering securities with the state available to companies already registered with the SEC, one of three ways provided by the Uniform Securities Act to register securities. Nonexempt securities must be registered in each state in which they will be sold. Because the states acknowledge that SEC registration sets high standards for companies, the company simply notifies the state administrator of its intent to sell a security. Not all states recognize registration by notification. *See also* registration by coordination, registration by qualification.

registration by qualification The most complex of the three methods of registering securities provided by the Uniform Securities Act. Nonexempt securities must be registered in each state in which they will be sold. Any security may be registered using this method, but all nonexempt securities that do not qualify for registration under another method must use it. *See also* registration by coordination; registration by notification.

registration statement A statement that must be registered with the SEC for every new equity and debt security. It discloses: the nature of the issuer's business; detailed financial information for the company; an explanation of how the proceeds from the sale will be used; names of key management personnel and directors, as well as their salaries, business history, and share of ownership in the company; information about other owners of ten percent or more of the company; and whether the company is involved in any legal proceedings. A prospectus must accompany this documentation. The SEC uses this information to determine whether to allow the offering to proceed.

regressive tax A flat rate tax, such as a five percent sales tax. Regressive taxes are hardest on the poor. *See also* progressive tax.

Reg T *See* Regulation T.

regular way settlement *See* settlement date.

Regulation A An amendment to the Securities Act of 1933 that allows issuers to raise up to $5 million from all securities within a 12-month period without going through the full registration process. In Regulation A offerings, the issuer files an offering circular instead of a prospectus and the cooling-off period is 20 days between the filing date and the effective date. Registered investment companies and oil or gas limited partnerships may not offer securities under Regulation A.

Regulation D An amendment to the Securities Act of 1933 dealing with registration requirements for issuers of securities. Regulation D defines, among other things, accredited investors, affiliates, aggregate offering prices, executive officers, and issuers. It also sets rules for calculation of number of purchasers.

Regulation G A regulation under the Securities Exchange Act of 1934 relating to extension of credit by lenders other than commercial banks. On April 1, 1998, Regulation U was amended to cover those lenders, thus eliminating Regulation G. *See also* Regulation U.

Regulation T (*generally known as* Reg T) A regulation under the Securities Exchange Act of 1934 that gives the Federal Reserve Board authority to regulate the buying of securities on credit (margin) and sets time limits within which clients must pay for purchases. Regulation T sets only initial requirements for opening a margin account and making the first purchase; NYSE and brokerage house requirements govern maintenance of the account. For a summary of margin requirements by type of security, *see* margin. *See also* Regulation T extension, settlement date.

Regulation T call Notification to an investor that a margin account has fallen below the equity required by Reg T, which is currently 50 percent. Reg T calls must be met within three business days or the firm may be forced to sell out the client's securities to cover the call. *See also* margin maintenance call, sell-out.

Regulation T extension Permission to pay for a trade after the settlement date. Three business days after trade date is the settlement date (T + 3). If after five business days (T+ 5) the amount due exceeds $500 and payment is not received, the broker must liquidate the position or request an extension. Reg T governs extensions of credit, which are granted by self-regulatory organizations such as the NASD. In case of a holiday, settlement and Reg T dates are extended. The chart below shows settlement and Reg T dates with and without a holiday. *See also* Regulation T, settlement date.

Trade Date (T) *with no holidays:*	Settlement Date (T + 3)	Regulation T Date (T + 5)
Monday, January 5	Thursday, January 8	Monday, January 12
If Monday, January 19 is a holiday:		
Monday, January 12	Thursday, January 15	Tuesday, January 21
Tuesday, January 13	Friday, January 16	Wednesday, January 22
Wednesday, January 14	Tuesday, January 20	Thursday, January 23
Thursday, January 15	Wednesday, January 21	Friday, January 26
Friday, January 16	Thursday, January 22	Monday, January 27
Tuesday, January 20	Friday, January 23	Tuesday, January 27

Regulation U A regulation pursuant to the Securities Exchange Act of 1934 pertaining to extension of credit for the purchase of securities. Reg U originally pertained to commercial banks only, but was amended in 1998 to cover all lenders.

rehypothecation The use of customer securities as collateral when a broker-dealer borrows money from a lender to finance customer debt. The firm may not pledge more securities than are needed to cover the amount of the loan. *See also* customer protection rule, hypothecation agreement, margin agreement.

reinvested earnings *See* retained earnings.

reinvestment Use of dividends or capital gains from stocks and mutual funds to buy additional shares rather than receiving the distributions in cash.

reinvestment risk The risk that when a bond comes due, falling interest rates will mean that the funds from the bond redemption will buy less in income. *Example:* An investor owns a $10,000 bond that pays five percent per year and matures in five years. At bond maturity, interest rates have fallen from five percent to 3.5 percent. The investor will have to reinvest the $10,000 at 3.5 percent, which will decrease income. *See also* risk.

REIT (real estate investment trust) A trust or corporation that pools professionally managed real estate investments. Income and profits pass through to investors in the form of dividends or capital gains distributions. REITs trade on exchanges and in the OTC market.

REMIC (real estate mortgage investment conduit) A company that pools investors' money to buy fixed portfolios of real estate investments. Like CMOs and REITs, REMICs pass income and gains through to investors. They may be issued as either debt (regular) or equity (residual) interests. Debt REMICs are like bonds, paying interest and principal from the underlying mortgages. Equity REMICs are like stock, paying dividends and capital gains. Unlike CMOs, REMICs offer investors alternatives for risk, principal balances, interest rates, average lives, prepayment characteristics, and final maturities so investors can find one that meets their unique needs for risk and maturity.

reoffering price The price at which a syndicate sells a new issue of municipal bonds to the public. The underwriter buys the bonds from the issuer at a discount, perhaps $980 on a bond it sells to the public for $1,000. The $20 difference, called the spread, goes to the underwriter. *See also* underwriting spread.

reorganization ("reorg") department The back office department responsible for handling any changes to securities held by the firm for clients, such as name changes due to mergers and acquisitions, quantity changes due to splits and reverse splits, or redemption of securities due to tender offers or calls.

repurchase agreement (repo) An agreement between a borrower (seller) and a lender (buyer) to do a transaction and then reverse it at a specified date and price. Repos are very short-term contracts. *Example:* A bank that needs cash has a large inventory of government bonds. The bank finds an investor that will buy them and agree to sell them back to the bank for a predetermined price. If the repurchase agreement specifies a date, it is called a fixed agreement. If the date is not specified, it is called an open repo and is callable at any time. The lender's interest rate is calculated into the price of the repurchase agreement. The Federal Reserve Bank often uses repos to make adjustments to the money supply. *See also* reverse repurchase agreement (reverse repo).

reserve requirement The minimum amount of reserves the Federal Reserve requires its member banks to maintain as a percentage of their deposits. For example, if the reserve requirement is ten percent, a member bank must deposit $10 at the Federal Reserve for every $100 in deposits that it holds. The other $90 is available for loan to other member banks needing to meet their reserve requirements. Many large banks loan out more than they take in in deposits and often need to borrow funds overnight to meet the reserve requirements. *See also* federal funds rate.

residual claim The claim a stockholder has to the assets of a corporation if it must be liquidated. Common stockholders have the lowest priority; their claims will be considered only after bondholders and preferred stockholders have been paid.

resistance The top of the trading range within which a stock price fluctuates for a period of time. Technical analysts believe the price of the stock goes up until it meets resistance, then drops. When stock prices reach their resistance levels, many stockholders sell, believing the price will drop. If the stock price rises above the resistance level, it is seen as a bullish event. *See also* support.

Resistance

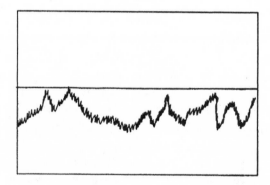

restricted account A margin account in which the equity has dropped between the 50 percent Regulation T (Reg T) initial margin requirement and the 25 percent minimum maintenance. When a margin account becomes restricted, the Reg T retention requirement prohibits clients from withdrawing securities without depositing cash or other securities with a value of 50 percent of whatever is being withdrawn. In essence, if the customer paid half of the initial purchase, the other half must be paid before the security can be withdrawn. A customer who buys additional shares in a restricted account must deposit cash or securities worth 50 percent of the purchase price of the new security. If an investor sells securities in a restricted account, Reg T retention requirements allow 50 percent of the proceeds to be paid to the client. Investors may withdraw all dividends and interest received from a restricted account.

restricted person According to the SEC, the term "restricted person" includes most associated persons of a member firm, most owners and affiliates of a broker-dealer, and certain other classes of persons (SEC). SEC Rule 2790 prohibits exchange members from selling a new issue to an account in which a restricted person has a beneficial interest. The rule eliminates the requirement that a new issue be "hot" and it now applies to all new issues. *See also* associated person.

restricted security A security that has been acquired directly or indirectly from the issuer or an affiliate of the issuer, in other words, not in a public offering. Examples of restricted stock are securities bought in a private placement, stock given to employees as part of compensation, or stock given in exchange for start-up capital for a new company. Restricted stock is exempt from registration; it carries a legend on the stock certificate that states that it is restricted. There is a mandatory one-year holding period for restricted securities. SEC Rule 144 regulates the sale of restricted stock. *See also* Rule 144.

retained earnings *(also called* reinvested earnings, earned surplus*)* The amount of a corporation's net income that remains after all dividends have been paid to preferred and common stockholders.

retained earnings ratio A comparison of retained earnings to net income available for common stock. The ratio is the complement to the dividend payout ratio. *See also* dividend payout ratio.

$$\frac{\text{Retained earnings}}{\text{Net income available to common stock}} = \text{Retained earnings ratio}$$

retention requirement The Reg T prohibition against client withdrawal of securities from a restricted margin account without depositing cash or other securities with a value of 50 percent of whatever is being withdrawn. If an investor sells securities in a restricted account, Reg T retention requirements allow 50 percent of the proceeds to be paid to the client. *See also* restricted account.

return on assets ratio A measure of a company's profitability relative to its total assets. The ratio shows earnings generated from invested capital.

$$\frac{\text{Net income}}{\text{Total assets}} = \text{Return on assets}$$

return on equity ratio A profitability measure that is useful in comparing companies in the same industry.

$$\frac{\text{Net income}}{\text{Shareholders' equity}} = \text{Return on equity}$$

revenue anticipation note (RAN) Short-term securities issued by municipalities. RANs are often issued if a municipality needs cash just before revenues from another source are to be received. Proceeds from the receipt of revenues repay the RAN holders. RANs are considered money market securities.

revenue bond A type of municipal bond with the following characteristics:
- Revenue bonds are backed by the income of a project or enterprise.
- Revenue bonds are used to fund capital projects that generate revenue, such as utilities, airports, or toll bridges.
- Principal and interest payments on revenue bonds are financed by fees or income from the project or enterprise.
- Revenue bonds do not require voter approval.
- Revenue bonds are not rated.
- New issues of revenue bonds are awarded through a negotiated underwriting.

See also general obligation (GO) bond.

reversal The end of an upward or downward trendline, when the price of a security moves the other way.

reverse repurchase agreement (reverse repo) A repurchase agreement in which the buyer and seller positions are reversed. *See also* repurchase agreement (repo).

reverse stock split A reduction in the number of shares outstanding with an increase in their price, used when the price of a stock is so low that it has become unattractive to investors or is in jeopardy of being delisted from its exchange. *Example:* ABC Corporation has fallen to $2 per share, so the company declares a one-for-five (1:5) reverse stock split. The company cancels all outstanding certificates and distributes one new share for every five old shares owned by investors. An investor who had owned 100 shares before the split would own 20 shares after, and the price of the stock would be increased to $10. The investor still has the same $200 market value in the stock. Since a stock split changes the par value of a stock, it must be approved in advance by shareholders. In a reverse stock split, because the number of shares outstanding are reduced, earnings per share increase. *See also* stock split, rights offering.

right The opportunity for current stockholders to buy shares of new common stock or securities convertible to common stock, sometimes at a discount, before they are sold to the public. Rights offerings usually last 30 to 45 days. During that time shareholders receive a subscription right certificate for the number of shares they are allowed to purchase. Shareholders have the following options:
   1. They may exercise their rights by turning in the subscription certificate and a check for the new shares.
   2. They may sell the right to someone else; rights are negotiable securities that trade on exchanges.
   3. They may allow the subscription right to expire at the end of the offering period.

Because rights trade for cash (same-day) settlement, the ex-rights date, or the day the stock trades without the rights, is the first business day after the effective date of the SEC registration statement. *See also* preemptive right, subscription right certificate, rights offering.

rights agent An agent similar to a transfer agent who keeps records of owners of rights and converts subscription right certificates into shares of common stock. *See also* right.

right of accumulation Use of the total value of an investor's accounts with a family of mutual funds to determine whether the sales charge should be reduced for later purchases. For example, an investor with two accounts totaling $50,000 in value may qualify for a reduced sales charge on subsequent purchases. *See also* breakpoint.

rights offering An offering to existing shareholders of the right to buy more stock before a new public offering. This distribution of rights gives shareholders the option of retaining proportionate ownership in the company. This is a typical rights offering notice:

"The rights offering will commence on February 10, 2003 and will expire on March 11, 2003. Holders of common stock of XYZ Corp. will receive, at no cost, 0.05 rights for each share of common stock they held at the close of business on February 7, 2003. Each whole right entitles the holder to purchase one share of common stock at a subscription price of $2.15. Rights holders who exercise their rights in full will also have the opportunity to subscribe for additional shares of common stock that are not purchased by other eligible rights holders."

A shareholder who owns 100 shares of stock may thus buy five additional shares (100 x .05 = 5) at $2.15 per new share, or $10.75. *See also* right.

risk The possibility of loss on an investment. Generally speaking, the higher the risk, the greater potential for return, as well as loss. However, in this dictionary alone, 20 types of risk are defined. They should all be considered carefully before investing. *See also* call risk, capital risk, country risk, credit risk, default risk, economic risk, financial risk, inflation risk, interest rate risk, legislative risk, liquidity risk, margin risk, marketability risk, market risk, nonsystematic risk, purchasing power risk, reinvestment risk, selection risk, systematic risk, timing risk.

risk arbitrage (*also called* takeover arbitrage) During corporate takeovers, the purchase of stock of the takeover target and the short sale of the stock of the acquirer. The belief is that the pending merger will raise the price of the company being acquired and lower the price of the acquirer's shares. *Example:* Shares of the target company are trading at $30 when the arbitrageur buys its shares and they begin to rise. The acquiring company's shares are trading at $40 when the arbitrageur sells its shares short and they begin to fall. If the takeover takes place, the target company's shares will be replaced by the acquiring company's shares and become the same issue. The arbitrageur has bought at $30 and sold at $40, making a profit of $10 a share. The reason this is called risk arbitrage is that if the merger does not take place, the arbitrageur must cover the short position, possibly at a huge loss. *See also* arbitrage.

riskless and simultaneous transactions Purchase or sale of a stock by a broker for its own account, followed by sale or purchase to the customer as principal, charging the markup or markdown according to the five percent policy. This happens when a broker-dealer has a client order to buy or sell a stock that it does not hold in its own inventory. Its other option would be to act as an agent for the client and go to a market maker, buy or sell on the client's behalf, and charge commission.

rollover *See* IRA rollover.

Roth IRA An IRA named for its architect, the late Senator William V. Roth, Jr., contributions to which are not tax-deductible, but distributions from which are tax-free once certain conditions are met. In 2005, the contribution limit for a Roth IRA is $4,000, or $4,500 for individuals age 50 and older. To avoid taxation, distributions must be made after the end of a five-year waiting period, and the account owner is age 59 1/2 or older, or disabled, or using the distribution to pay first-time home-buying expenses up to $10,000, or is a beneficiary of the deceased account owner. All dividends, income and capital gains accumulate tax free. Roth IRAs can be set up with a bank or brokerage firm. *See also* IRA.

round lot The standard unit of securities trading, 100 shares of stock on major exchanges or a bond with a face value of $1,000 or $5,000. *See also* odd lot.

RR *See* registered representative.

Rule 15c3-3 The SEC rule spelling out the obligation of the seller to deliver the securities that have been sold. If the security that was sold from a long position is not delivered by ten days after settlement date, the broker must buy the customer in or request an extension.

Rule 80A *See* collars.

Rule 80B *See* circuit breakers.

Rule 144 The SEC rule that allows shareholders who own restricted or control stock to sell the shares to the public after a number of conditions are met. The purpose of Rule 144 is to prevent a public market in securities where adequate information about the company is not available to the public. Restricted and control stock has a statement on the face of the certificate that says that the shares cannot be sold unless they are registered with the SEC or are exempt from the registration requirements. This legend must be removed by the transfer agent before the shares can be sold; but the transfer agent needs the approval of the issuer before the legend can be removed and a clean certificate issued. Before restricted stock can be sold, Form 144 must be filed with the SEC detailing information about the issuer, the shareholder, how and when the shares were acquired, and whether securities of the same issue were sold by the shareholder within the previous three months. A thorough explanation of Rule 144 can be found at www.sec.gov. *See also* control security, restricted security.

Rule 405 *See* Know Your Customer Rule.

Rules of Fair Practice *See* NASD Manual.

Russell Equity Indexes The 21 U.S. stock indexes published by the Frank Russell Company (*see* www.russell.com). The Russell 3000 index "measures the performance of the 3,000 largest U.S. companies based on total market capitalization, which represents approximately 98 percent of the investable U.S. equity market." The Russell 2000 Index is the most widely quoted measure of the small- to mid-cap market; it measures the performance of the 2,000 smallest companies in the Russell 3000 Index, and represents approximately eight percent of the total market capitalization of the Russell 3000 Index.

safe harbor SEC rules that allow management to publicly discuss a company's future plans and financial projections without fear of lawsuits from investors as long as the statements are made in good faith.

safekeeping The option of having stock and bond certificates registered in the client's name but held in the broker-dealer's vault. Dividends and interest are sent to the client's address of record or reinvested. When a client sells a security that is held in safekeeping, all registered owners must sign a stock or bond power to make the security negotiable. *See* also street name.

sales charge *See* load.

Sallie Mae *See* Student Loan Marketing Association.

same-day settlement Trades entered for cash, outside the regular procedures (except that some securities automatically settle on the same day as trade date, among them rights and money market instruments bought and sold in large institutional accounts). Same-day settlement trades are negotiated with a premium charged to the buyer and a discount to the seller. NYSE rules and NASD Uniform Practices Code require that cash settlements be made by 2:30 p.m. EST. If a cash trade takes place after 2:00 p.m. EST, settlement must be within 30 minutes. *See also* settlement date.

Sarbanes-Oxley Act of 2002 Federal legislation passed in response to the failures of major U.S. corporations due to questionable accounting practices, poor management, and lack of internal controls, designed to protect investor's ownership of companies by requiring accurate and reliable disclosures by corporate management and directors. The act established the Public Company Accounting Oversight Board, mandated independent corporate auditors, increased corporate responsibility for financial reports, enhanced financial disclosures, required codes of ethics for senior officers, set rules on conflicts of interest of securities analysts, and increased penalties for criminal, corporate and white-collar fraud.

savings bond Securities issued by the U.S. Treasury and backed by the full faith and credit of the United States government. They can be bought at commercial banks or at Treasury Direct, at a discount or face value, depending on the series of bond. Savings bonds are nonmarketable, that is, ownership cannot be transferred from one owner to another and they can be redeemed only by the registered owner or beneficiary. Interest earned on savings bonds is subject to federal but not state or local income taxes. *See also* Series EE bond, Series HH bond, Series I bond.

secondary distribution A type of block trade reserved for only the largest blocks of stock. Nonmember firms may be asked to join NYSE member firms to participate. The price quoted is net to the buyer. The seller pays all fees and commissions. The trade is not shown on the Tape, but is included in the day's price and volume figures after the close of the market. Shares are not presented to the floor but trade after the close at a price that may not be higher than the closing price. This is not to be confused with a secondary offering, which involves underwriting and a prospectus. *See also* block trade.

secondary market The exchanges, such as the NYSE, and the over-the-counter market, where investors buy and sell securities from each other through stockbrokers or online trading.

secondary offering The offering by one or more stockholders, rather than the company, to sell all or a large portion of their shares. A prospectus is required and the proceeds go to the selling stockholders. The offered shares can be new or additional issues. This is not to be confused with a secondary distribution, which is a type of block trade. *See also* primary offering, split offering.

SEC fee A small fee, only cents per 100 shares sold, which is separate from commissions or other charges, payable to the SEC as a means of recovering government costs of regulating securities markets. Broker-dealers collect the fee on sales transactions and forward the proceeds to the NASD or exchanges, who pass it on to the SEC and the U.S. Treasury.

Section 529 plan *See* 529 plan.

sector An industry grouping of companies generally in the same business, such as automobiles and components; hotel, restaurant and leisure; retail; telecommunications and capital goods.

Securities Act of 1933 Federal legislation enacted after the crash of 1929 to govern the issuance of new securities. The act ensures that potential investors are fully informed about securities and the companies that issue them before they are sold to the public. Issuers are required to register them with the federal government, provide for thorough disclosure of information to investors by way of a prospectus, and are prohibited from making misrepresentations either directly or through underwriters. Certain securities, such as federal, state, and local bonds, and offerings, such as private placements and some corporate offerings, are exempt from the act. *See also* Glass-Steagall Act of 1933, Maloney Act, Regulation A, Regulation D, Securities Exchange Act of 1934.

Securities Acts Amendments of 1975 A law amending the Securities Exchange Act of 1934 by ending fixed commission rates, calling for the establishment of a national stock market system and an updated clearance and settlement system; granting the SEC more authority over SROs; and establishing the Municipal Securities Rulemaking Board (MSRB).

Securities and Exchange Commission (SEC) The federal government agency established by the Securities Exchange Act of 1934 to protect investors and maintain the integrity of securities markets by enforcing the Securities Act of 1933 and the Securities Exchange Act of 1934, as well as later regulation. Its five commissioners are appointed by the president of the United States. The SEC monitors securities, stock exchanges, broker-dealers, investment advisors, mutual funds, and public utility holding companies. *For more information*, see www.sec.gov. *See also* Securities Act of 1933, Securities Exchange Act of 1934.

Securities Exchange Act of 1934 Federal legislation that established the SEC to enforce federal laws affecting securities and to oversee trading of securities in the secondary market. It provides for registration of securities traded on stock exchanges; oversight of stock exchanges, brokerage firms, transfer agents, and clearing agencies; periodic reporting of information by publicly traded companies; disclosure of material contained in proxy solicitations to shareholders; disclosure by investors seeking to own five percent or more of a company's stock through direct purchase or tender offers; regulation of insider trading and short sales; the customer protection rule; the net capital rule, and disciplinary and enforcement powers over regulated agencies and individuals. The act also empowered the Federal Reserve Board to regulate the extension of credit for purchasing securities. The Maloney Act of 1938 broadened the Securities Exchange Act of 1934 by establishing the NASD to regulate the over-the-counter market. *See also* Regulation G, Regulation T, Regulation U.

Securities Investor Protection Corporation *See* SIPC.

security Any investment instrument, such as a stock, bond, option contract, right, or warrant. It can represent ownership in a company, as in stocks; a position as a creditor, as in bonds; or rights to ownership, such as options, rights, or warrants.

security arbitrage Arbitrage involving equivalent securities, such as convertible bonds and common stock. *Example:* a $1,000 convertible bond has a conversion price of $25, which would give the owner 40 shares of common stock ($1,000 ÷ $25 = 40 shares). An arbitrageur would buy the bonds for $1,000 each, convert them to common stock, expecting the stock price to go higher than $25 so he can sell the stock for a profit. *See also* arbitrage.

selection risk The possibility that a client's choice of security, no matter how much research has been done, may be wrong because of a decline in sector or company value. *See also* risk.

self-regulatory organization (SRO) Organizations, such as the NYSE, AMEX, and NASD, that make rules to ensure market integrity and protection of investors and discipline improper conduct by their members. SRO rules must be approved by the SEC.

seller's option contract Sale of a security with the stipulation that the seller need not deliver the security to the buyer until 6 business days to 60 calendar days after trade date. The seller must give the buyer one day's notice before delivery of the security.

selling away The offer by a broker of an investment that is outside the firm's regular business. For example, a broker may offer a client gold coins, which her firm does not sell. This is considered a private securities transaction, which is against SRO rules and federal securities laws.

selling concession *See* underwriting spread.

selling dividends A broker's recommendation to buy mutual funds just before a capital gains distribution, which is prohibited because as soon as the capital gains are paid, the price of the fund will drop by the amount of the distribution, and the distribution will be taxable.

selling group Brokerage firms that help members of underwriting syndicates to sell a large new issue to the public. Because they are not members of the syndicate, they do not have the same obligation as syndicate members to buy the security. *See also* underwriters.

selling short *See* short sale.

selling to cover Buying a security in a cash account and selling it without having paid for it. The account of an investor who does this is immediately frozen for 90 days, during which securities may be bought and sold but only on a cash-in-advance basis, and stocks must be long in the account before they can be sold.

sell-out (1) Action taken when a broker-dealer on the buy side of the transaction fails to pay for securities purchased. If after ten days the buying broker-dealer has not settled with the seller, the seller may execute a sell-out to complete the trade, and charge the buying broker-dealer, regardless of the price. (2) Similarly, the sale by a broker of the securities of a client who has not honored a margin call. The firm is not required to contact the customer before a forced sell-out, or extend the time a client has to meet either a Reg T call or maintenance call. If a broker must sell securities to cover a Reg T call, the client's account must be frozen for 90 days. *See also* frozen account.

sell stop order An order that protects shareholder profits or prevents further losses if the price of the stock should drop. Stop orders become market orders once the stock trades at or through a price set by the shareholder, called the stop price. *Example:* An investor bought 1,000 shares of Avon at $55, and the stock is now selling at $65. The investor enters a stop order to sell 1,000 Avon at $62 stop. If the price drops to $62, the order is triggered and becomes a market order. Stop orders do not guarantee that the stock will sell at $62; with a market order, the shares sell at the highest available bid price, which in a rapidly declining market could be considerably lower than $62. Stop orders are accepted on all major exchanges, but not over the counter. *See also* buy stop orders, sell stop orders, stop limit orders.

senior security Securities that have the prior claim on assets if a company must be liquidated: Bondholders are senior to both preferred and common stockholders; preferred stockholders are senior to common stockholders.

SEP *See* simplified employee pension (SEP) plan.

serial bond A bond issued with a maturity schedule in which the parts of the issue are redeemed in stages over a period of years. Serial bonds are quoted on a yield basis, rather than by price. *See also* term bond.

serial maturity The schedule of stages an issuer sets for when serial bonds mature. *See also* balloon maturity, term maturity.

series All options in the same class with the same exercise price and expiration month. *Example:* All Microsoft April $27.50 calls are in one series, all Microsoft April $30 calls in another.

series bond A bond issued in stages and sold at intervals over a period of time.

Series EE bond The Treasury securities, issued since 1980, that replaced the Series E bonds that were issued from May 1941 through June 1980. Series EE savings bonds are accrual bonds; they are bought at a discount of 50 percent of face value and do not pay interest until maturity: A $100 bond that costs $50 is redeemed for $100 at maturity. Denominations of $50 through $10,000 are available.

The Treasury has separate rate and time schedules for Series EE bonds bought before May 1995, those bought between May 1995 and April 1997, and those bought in May 1997 or later. For the last group, May 1997 and after, interest is adjusted every six months based on 90 percent of the average yield of the five-year Treasury security. As a result, maturity dates fluctuate. If interest rates should drop so low that a bond does not reach face value after 17 years, the Treasury will make a one-time adjustment to bring the bond to face value at that time. After EE bonds reach face value, they earn interest until they are redeemed or reach a final maturity of 30 years. *See also* Patriot Bond.

Series HH bond The Treasury securities that replaced Series H bonds, which were sold from June 1952 through December 1979. Series HH savings bonds are current-income securities; they are issued at face value and pay interest every six months over the life of the bond. They cannot be bought with cash; they are available only in exchange for Series EE/E bonds or by reinvestment of the pro-ceeds of matured Series H bonds. They are available in denominations of $500 through $10,000.

Series I bond Inflation-adjusted savings bonds issued by the U.S. Treasury. They are accrual bonds; interest is added to the bond monthly and paid when the bond is redeemed. Series I bonds sell at face value; for example, a $100 bond costs $100. Eight denominations of $50 through $30,000 are available. Series I bonds earn interest for up to 30 years, calculated using a combination of fixed and vari-able rates: the fixed rate of return remains the same throughout the life of the bond but there is an additional variable inflation rate that is adjusted every six months based on the Consumer Price Index for Urban Consumers (CPI-U).

series issue A time schedule an issuer sets for sales of new bonds at intervals over a period of time.

Series 6 license The license held by NASD broker-dealers who have passed the Series 6 Investment Company Products/Variable Contracts Representative examination, allowing them to sell securities issued under the Investment Company Act of 1940, such as mutual funds and unit investment trusts, and new issues of closed-end funds, variable annuities, and insurance products.

Series 7 license The license held by NASD broker-dealers who have passed the Series 7 General Securities Representative Examination, the most in-depth test for brokers and a prerequisite for NASD's many principal examinations. Holders of the Series 7 license may sell all types of securities (corporate stocks, bonds, and options; U.S. government and government agency securities; municipal securities; mutual funds, variable contracts and direct participation programs) except for commodity futures, which requires the Series 3 license. For a com-plete list of NASD licenses, *see* www.nasdr.com/5200_explan.asp.

Series 11 license The license acquired by passing the Series 11 Assistant Representative–Order Processing examination that allows sales assistants to accept unsolicited orders from clients. It does not permit the holder to accept orders for municipal securities or direct participation programs or be compen-sated by commissions or bonuses based on orders or accounts opened.

Series 52 license The license acquired by passing the Series 52 Municipal Securities Representative examination attesting to the fact that the holder is familiar with U.S. government and government agency securities, economics, interest rates, government policy, and federal securities law.

Series 62 license The license acquired by passing the Series 62 Corporate

Securities Limited Representative examination that qualifies an NASD broker-dealer to sell corporate stocks, bonds, rights and warrants; real estate investment trusts (REITs); collateralized mortgage obligations (CMOs); and securities issued under the Investment Company act of 1940, such as mutual funds and unit investment trusts.

Series 63 license The license acquired by passing the NASD Series 63 Uniform Securities Agent State Law Examination, which covers state licensing and registration issues, as well as fraudulent and other prohibited practices. *See also* blue-sky laws.

settlement Completion of the transaction. At settlement, the buyer pays for purchased securities and the seller delivers the securities that have been sold.

settlement date The date on which the trade must be paid and ownership changes. For most securities, this is on the third business day after trade date (T+3). For example, if a client purchases stock on Monday, January 12 (trade date), settlement date is Thursday, January 15. For some securities, such as options and U.S. Government notes and bonds, regular way settlement is the next day. T-notes bought on January 12 would thus settle on January 13. For other securities, such as money market instruments (CDs, T-bills, commercial paper, and banker's acceptances) purchased in large institutional accounts, regular way settlement is the same day as the trade date. In smaller retail accounts, regular way for money market investments is next day. *See also* Regulation T extension, same-day settlement.

Type of Security	Trade Date	Settlement Date
Most stocks and bonds	January 12	January 15
Options, U.S. government notes and bonds	January 12	January 13
T-bills, CDs, money markets (institutional)	January 12	January 12
T-bills, CDs, money markets (retail)	January 12	January 13

shareholders' equity (*also called* net worth) The amount of a company's capital that was financed through the sale of common and preferred stock, representing what stockholders could claim against a company's assets. On balance sheets there are usually three items under this heading: capital stock at par, capital in excess of par, and retained earnings. *Capital stock at par* is the par value of all common and preferred stock outstanding. If the company has outstanding one million shares of common stock with a par value of $1, capital stock at par would be $1 million. *Capital in excess of par* represents the money received from a stock offering over and above the $1 par value. If the company sold one million shares of new stock with a par value of $1 for $6 per share, $1 million would go to capital stock at par and the other $5 would be capital in excess of par. *Retained earn - ings* are profits that have not been paid out as dividends.

shares of beneficial interest *See* beneficial interest.

shelf registration Registration documents filed with the SEC pursuant to SEC Rule 415 for stocks or bonds to be issued at some time over the next two years. In most securities offerings, all stocks or bonds are sold at one time and the company receives the proceeds of the sale all at once, but some corporations prefer to spread their offering out over time. With the registration "on the shelf", the company can decide the best time to offer the securities to the public. *Example:* Avnet Inc. filed registration documents with the SEC for a shelf offering that allowed the company occasionally to sell up to a total of $1.5 billion in debt securities, common stocks, and other securities.

short against the box Transactions used before the 1997 revisions of the Internal Revenue Code to postpone capital gains: if a client owned stock and instructed the broker to sell the same stock short, the client was short against the box. *Example:* Investor Y owns 500 shares of AT&T. Y asked the broker to sell short 500 AT&T; rather than delivering her own shares, Y borrowed 500 shares from the brokerage firm, ending up long 500 shares and short 500 shares. The strategy was to postpone capital gains by creating a neutral position: she had losses (in the short stock) equal to gains (in the long stock). To close the position, Y could either deliver the long shares or buy new stock to cover the short position. However, the 1997 tax code revisions virtually eliminated the short-against-the-box strategy.

short-interest theory The theory held by some technical analysts that if a large number of shares have been sold short, they will have to be repurchased, so there is likely to be a rise in the price of the stock as short positions are covered.

short position The securities borrowed from and thus owed back to a brokerage firm by investors who sell short. *See* short sale.

	Long Position	Short Position
Opening transaction	Buy low	Sell high (Borrow securities from brokerage firm)
Closing transaction	Sell high	Buy low (buy back securities to replace securities borrowed).

short sale A strategy for making a profit in a declining market. The investor borrows shares of stock from a broker-dealer and sells them, in the belief that the price of the security will drop in value. If the strategy works, the investor can buy it back at a lower price and make a profit on the difference (minus costs). If the strategy does not work and the price of the security goes up, the investor may need a lot of money to buy the stock back. Orders to sell short on an exchange may be executed only on a plus-tick or zero-plus-tick.

Short sales must be executed in a margin account and are subject to Reg T margin requirements. For short sales, Reg T requires 150 percent of the current market value of the security, the first 100 percent being the proceeds from the sale of the stock and the rest being deposited by the investor. *Example:* Investor X sells short 500 shares of a $25 stock. The margin requirements would be:

	Proceeds from the sale	Reg T (50%)	Cash required
Sell short 500 XYZ Corp. at $25	$12,500	$6,250	$18,750

The reason so much cash is required for a short sale is the risk, which is unlimited if the price of the securities goes up. X would have to keep 150 percent of the stock's value in the margin account until he buys the stock to close the position. *See also* margin, plus-tick, Regulation T, zero-plus-tick.

short straddle The sale of a call and a put on the same underlying stock with the same strike price and expiration date, such as sale of Cisco Mar 20 calls and Cisco Mar 20 puts.

short-term capital gain The gain on the sale of a capital asset, such as securities, real estate, or tangible property, that has been held for one year or less.

short-term capital loss The loss on the sale of a capital asset, such as securities, real estate, or tangible property, that has been held for one year or less.

signature guarantee Authentication to a transfer agent by an exchange member firm or a bank of the endorsements (signatures) of sellers on stock certificates or a stock or bond power.

SIMPLE IRA Salary-reduction retirement plans may be offered by small businesses to their employees. In 2005 employees may elect to have up to 100 percent of annual compensation contributed to a SIMPLE IRA, up to $10,000 per participant ($12,000 for employees age 50 or older). A SIMPLE IRA may be offered only through an employer, who may set it up at a bank or brokerage firm. *See also* IRA.

simplified employee pension (SEP) plan An IRA to which both an employer and an employee can contribute. For 2005 the employer may contribute up to 25 percent of the employee's compensation, or $42,000, whichever is less. SEPs are suited to small businesses and self-employed individuals. They must cover all employees age 21 and older who earned over $450 (in 2004), and who have worked for the employer at any time during at least three of the past five years. A SEP is offered only through an employer, who may set it with a bank or brokerage firm. *See also* IRA.

single account An account that has only one beneficial owner, whose name is on the account and who is the only person who may buy or sell securities or request distributions of cash or securities from the account.

sinking fund An account set up by issuers of bonds or preferred stock in which to accumulate money to call the securities, buy them back in the open market, or redeem them at maturity. Securities supported by sinking funds are perceived to be safer than those without them.

SIPC (Securities Investor Protection Corporation) An independent corporation, sponsored by the U.S. government, that was created by the Securities Investor Protection Act of 1970 to settle customer claims in the event of closure of a brokerage firm due to bankruptcy or other financial difficulties. All brokerage firms registered with the SEC are members and must pay into the SIPC general insurance fund. In case of brokerage failure, a court-appointed trustee would manage liquidation of a brokerage firm's assets first by delivering to the clients all securities registered in customer name and then by distributing all remaining customer assets (stocks and bonds held in street name and cash) to the firm's clients pro rata. SIPC reserve funds are used to make up any difference, up to a ceiling of $500,000 *per customer*, including $100,000 for cash claims. For purposes of the limit, all accounts in one customer's name are aggregated. *Example:* John Smith's cash account and IRA are considered one account. John Smith and Jane Smith JTWROS is a separate account, as is John Smith Custodian for Sally Smith. Corporate, partnership, and trust accounts are considered separate customers.

The SIPC does not reimburse clients if they lose money in the stock or bond markets. Commodity futures contracts and currency are ineligible for SIPC protection. *For more information*: www.sipc.org.

SMA *See* special memorandum account.

Small Order Execution System (SOES) An automatic order execution system used by NASDAQ member firms to facilitate trading of orders less than or equal to 1,000 shares (200 shares or less for stocks with low volume). The SOES began in 1984 but was made mandatory after the 1987 market crash, when sell orders from small investors went unfilled. SOES now gives small investors equal access to markets and order execution.

socially responsible investing The philosophy that investors should buy securities of corporations that contribute to the welfare of society by supporting education, the arts, and the underprivileged; protecting the environment; avoiding military enterprise, and displaying high ethical values. Several mutual funds screen companies for those qualities.

sole proprietorship The form of business ownership that has only one owner who makes all management decisions.

solicited order An order that was recommended to the investor by the registered representative. Order tickets to buy or sell securities include a place to mark the trade as solicited or unsolicited. Regulatory agencies and brokerage firms are paying more attention to the solicited/unsolicited status of orders because some brokers were mismarking order tickets as unsolicited when in fact the trades were solicited.

special bid *See* special offering.

special cash account *See* cash account.

special offering A type of block trade used to sell larger blocks; any number of NYSE member firms may be involved. An announcement is made on the Consolidated Tape before the transaction, showing the net price. The trade is presented to the floor of the exchange during market hours. All costs and commissions are paid by the initiator of the trade. Member firms may purchase for their own accounts or those of their clients. Partial completions are reported on the Tape at the day's close of business. Special offerings are rarely executed because they take considerable time.

On the buy side is the *special bid*, in which the originating firm wishes to purchase shares and asks other firms to help find sellers. Otherwise, the trade is handled and reported like a special offering. *See also* block trade.

specialist Traders on the floor of an exchange who are responsible for maintaining a fair and orderly market in specific securities. Most specialists are responsible for five to ten stocks. Specialists manage the auction, act as dealer when they execute orders for their own accounts, act as broker when they execute orders left with them by other traders, and may buy or sell against the market to reduce price volatility. *See also* specialist unit.

specialist block trade A purchase or sale of a large quantity of stock that is handled by the specialist. Specialist block trades are not shown on the Consolidated Tape but are reported to the exchange. *See also* block trade.

specialist's book A record of stock in inventory, limit and stop orders, and other orders that brokers have placed with the specialist.

specialist short-sale ratio A comparison of the number of short sales made by specialists and the total number of short sales transacted on the market. This is a good indicator of the mood of the market; a high number (60 percent or more) is bearish, because specialists seem to be expecting prices to drop, and a low number (45 percent or less) is bullish. *See also* selling short, specialist.

specialist unit An independent company employing specialists that contracts with the exchanges. On the NYSE, 7 firms employ 443 specialists who handle more than 2,800 stocks. *See also* specialist.

special memorandum account (SMA) An account created when a margin account has excess equity. No cash or securities are transferred to an SMA account; it is simply a line of credit that can be used for cash withdrawals or security purchases or withdrawals. SMA may be generated in several ways:

- An increase in the value of securities held in the account,
- A deposit of cash to the account that is not required for a margin call,
- Dividend and interest earnings on securities in the account,
- A deposit of securities to the account that is not required for a margin call.

Example: Investor G buys on margin 500 shares of stock at $50 ($25,000) and deposits the Reg T 50 percent minimum ($12,500). The account looks like this:

$25,000	Market value long
-12,500	Debit balance
12,500	Equity
-12,500	Reg T (50% of purchase)
0	Excess equity
0	SMA

If the value of each share increases to $55, the excess equity can be withdrawn as cash, used to purchase more stock, or credited to SMA:

$27,500	Market value long
-12,500	Debit balance
15,000	Equity
-12,500	Reg T (50% of purchase)
2,500	Excess equity
2,500	SMA

If the value of a share thereafter decreases to $45, the market value goes down, the debit balance remains the same, the client's equity declines, Reg T remains the same, there is no excess equity, but the SMA does not change. Once there is a credit to an SMA, it stays there even if the value of the securities declines. Only withdrawal of funds or purchase or withdrawal of securities will change it.

$22,500	Market value long
-12,500	Debit balance
10,000	Equity
-12,500	Reg T (50% of purchase)
0	Excess equity
2,500	SMA

speculation The assumption of high risk in the hope of a high return on an investment. For some sophisticated investors, it may be appropriate to speculate, using hedging strategies like options, futures, and stop loss orders to limit potential losses. Speculation is not for inexperienced investors or the faint of heart.

speculative bond *(also called* high-yield, junk, or non-investment grade bond) Risky bonds rated BB or lower by Standard & Poors or Ba or lower by Moody's The yields are high to offset the risk. *See also* bond rating.

split offering *(also called* a combined distribution) A combination of a primary and a secondary offering, with some of the new stock offered by the issuer and the rest by one or more shareholders. *See also* primary offering, secondary offering.

spot market A market in which goods are traded for immediate delivery and immediate payment. Examples of goods that trade in the spot market are commodities like grains, beef, coffee, oil, or foreign currency.

spot price The current price at which goods trade at a specific time and place. A spot price can be at a date in the future, for example, the spot price of euros at Bundesbank one year from today.

spot trade The purchase and sale of a commodity for cash for immediate delivery.

spousal IRA An IRA to which non-working as well as working spouses may contribute up to $4,000 ($4,500 if age 50 or older). The only requirements are that the couple be under the age of 70 1/2 and file a joint tax return, and that the working spouse earn income equal to or greater than the amount of the contribution. Whether the contribution is tax deductible depends on the couple's modified AGI. *See also* IRA.

spread (1) The purchase of one option and the sale of another in the same class (calls or puts on the same underlying security). A call spread is a long call and a short call. A put spread is a long put and a short put. Investors may create horizontal (time or calendar) spreads, vertical (price) spreads, or diagonal spreads. *See also* diagonal spread, calendar spread, price spread. (2) In quotations, the difference between the bid and the offer. A typical quote is Bid 56, Offered 56.125; the difference of $0.125 is the spread. *See also* offer, bid, underwriting spread.

Option	Strike Price	Calls - Last Trade			Puts - Last Trade		
		Jan	Feb	Mar	Jan	Feb	Mar
ABC	20	9.200	10.000	11.200	0.050	0.250	0.450
	22.50	6.700	9.250	10.875	0.050	0.300	0.400
	25	4.200	6.000	8.375	.0500	0.350	0.500
	27.50	1.900	2.350	4.750	0.200	0.750	1.275
	30	0.450	0.900	1.375	1.200	2.250	3.875
	32.50	0.050	0.800	10.250	3.200	5.500	6.250

Horizontal spread   Vertical spread   Diagonal spread

SRO *See* self-regulatory organization.

stabilizing Purchase of a new issue by members of the underwriting syndicate to help support (stabilize) the price if there is not much demand for the stock.

stagflation A term coined in the 1970s by economists trying to describe the combination of slow growth and high unemployment (stagnation) and rising prices (inflation). During times of stagflation, attempts to stimulate the economy and lower unemployment will increase inflation even more.

standardized option *See* listed option.

Standard & Poor's Corporation (S&P) A subsidiary of The McGraw-Hill Companies that is a leading provider of financial information for investors. Standard & Poor's provides credit ratings on corporate and municipal debt, equity and bond research through a number of well-known publications, and valuable benchmarks through its indexes. Its best-known index is the S&P 500, which lists 500 prominent companies in major industries in the United States. Although it is not as widely quoted as the Dow Jones Industrial Average, many investors favor the S&P 500 because its broad coverage better reflects the total market. A fascinating look at the S&P 500 can be found at SmartMoney's Map of the Market at www.smartmoney.com.
More information: www.standardandpoors.com.

standby underwriting (*also called* standby offering) The service offered to an issuer by an investment banker that is willing to buy stock of a new issue that has not been absorbed by current stockholders exercising rights and to sell it to the public. *See also* rights offering.

stated yield *See* coupon yield.

statement of intention *See* letter of intent.

state registration *See* Blue-Sky Laws, registration by coordination, registration by notification, registration by qualification.

statutory disqualification Ineligibility by law for employment with a member firm due to violations of NASD rules. Among the violations listed are some misdemeanor offenses and all felony criminal convictions (ineligible for ten years from the date of conviction); court rulings involving illegal investment activities; suspension or expulsion from an SRO; bars and suspensions ordered by the SEC or an SRO; denial or revocation of registration by the SEC or the CFTC (Commodity Futures Trading Commission); and making false statements in applications and reports to or proceedings before an SRO.

statutory voting rights One method of shareholder voting. When a board of directors is elected, each shareholder is entitled to one vote for each share owned, times the number of candidates; if there are five candidates, an owner of 100 shares will cast 500 votes. In the statutory method, the shareholder may assign no more than 100 votes to each director; if fewer than 100 votes are cast to one director, the remaining votes may not be assigned to another candidate. This method of voting favors majority stockholders. *See also* cumulative voting rights.

sticky issue A stock brought to market in an IPO for which there is not much investor demand; the opposite of a hot issue. The price of a sticky issue often drops when trading begins. During the underwriting period the managing underwriter may buy shares to help stabilize the price. *See also* hot issue, stabilizing, initial public offering (IPO).

stock A certificate evidencing ownership in a company; each share of stock represents a unit of equity in the company. Corporations issue stock in order to raise capital. *Example:* If a company issues 100,000 shares of stock, a shareholder who owns 1,000 shares owns one percent of the company. Stock can be purchased in an IPO or later from other shareholders in the secondary market. *See* also authorized stock, common stock, issued stock, outstanding stock, preferred stock, treasury stock, unissued stock.

stock ahead A situation where a limit order at a specific price is not filled because other orders at the same price were entered first. *Example:* A specialist received orders for XYZ Corp. stock in the following order: 1,000 @ 25; 500 @ 25; 200 @ 25. The price of XYZ Corp. may reach 25 long enough for the first two limit orders to be executed, but not the third.

stockbroker *See* registered representative.

stock certificate A document that confirms an individual's ownership in a corporation; an investor who buys 100 shares of stock will receive a certificate for 100 shares. A stock certificate lists the name of the corporation, number of shares, class of stock, CUSIP number, certificate number, name of the transfer agent, and the name of the registered owner. A stock certificate that is lost or stolen can be replaced by the transfer agent.

stock dividend The distribution of a company's net profits to shareholders in the form of shares of company stock. Each shareholder receives the same percentage of stock: if a five percent stock dividend is declared, a shareholder who owns 100 shares will receive a dividend of five shares, and a shareholder who owns 1,000 shares will receive 50 shares. This way the proportion of ownership in the company does not change. If shareholders are entitled to a fractional share of stock, they are usually mailed a check for the value of the fractional share.

Ex-dividend dates for stock dividends are different than for cash dividends. For stocks, the ex-dividend date is the first business day after the payable date. The reason for this is to avoid the price markdowns that would occur if the schedule was the same as for cash dividends. *See also* ex-dividend date.

stockholders' equity *See* shareholders' equity.

stock power A form used to transfer stock from one owner to another. It contains the same information as is on the back of a stock certificate. The advantage of using a stock power is safety: the stock power can be sent to the transfer agent separately from the stock certificate, reducing the risk of theft. *See also* assignment.

stock split The expansion of the number of outstanding shares of stock into a larger number, usually declared by a company when the price of its stock has gone so high it has become too expensive for many investors. *Example*: ABC Corporation declares a two-for-one (2:1) split for its stock because it is trading at $100 per share. The company distributes one additional share for each share outstanding; the owner of 100 shares before the split would own 200 shares after it. The stock price after the split is reduced proportionally to $50, so the investor still has the same market value in the stock: $10,000. If a proposed stock split leads to a change in a company's authorized shares or par value as outlined in the corporate charter, shareholder approval is required. In a 2:1 stock split, the number of shares outstanding are doubled, so EPS would decrease by half.

In the specialist's order book, prices are reduced when stocks split. Orders entered below the market price, such as buy limit, sell stop, and sell stop limit, are reduced on the ex-dividend date. Adjusted prices are calculated in the following example:

Original stock price = $100 per share
Stock split = 3 for 2
100 divided by 3/2 = 66.66
Adjusted order price = $66.00 per share

See also limit order, reverse stock split, stop order.

stop limit order A stop order that becomes a limit order when triggered. Like stop orders, stop limit orders protect shareholder profits or prevent further losses if the price of the stock drops. Unlike a stop order, which becomes a market order when triggered, stop limit orders become limit orders, which gives the shareholder more control over the execution price. *Example*: Investor K bought 500 shares of Cox Radio at $22; it is now $26 per share. K enters a stop limit order to sell 500 Cox Radio at $25 stop, limit $24.50. If the price drops to $25, K's order will be triggered as a limit order and will be executed at $24.50 or better. The stop limit order guarantees a minimum price. If the price drops quickly below $24.50, the trade will not be executed. Stop limit orders are accepted on all major exchanges, but not over the counter. *See* also limit order, stop order.

stop loss order *See* stop order.

stop order An order specifying a sales price that protects shareholder profits or prevents further losses if the price of the stock drops. Stop orders become market orders once the stock trades at or through a predetermined price, called the stop price. *Example:* Investor M bought 500 shares of Cox Radio at $22 a share; it is now selling at $26. M enters a stop order to sell 500 Cox Radio at $25 stop. If the price drops to $25, M's order will be triggered as a market order and executed. Stop orders do not guarantee a minimum price for the client; as a market order, the shares sell at the highest available bid price, which in a fast market could be considerably lower than $25. Stop orders are accepted on all major exchanges, but not over the counter. *See also* buy stop orders, sell stop orders, stop limit orders.

stopping stock A declaration by a specialist to guarantee a market order's bid or offer while the originating broker works to get a better price; the client will not pay any more on a purchase or receive any less on a sale. If the price begins to move away from the client, the specialist will execute the order at the stopped price.

straddle The purchase or sale of a call and a put on the same underlying stock with the same strike price and expiration date. A long straddle is the purchase of a call and a put, such as the purchase of Eastman Kodak Jan 15 calls and Jan 15 puts. A short straddle is the sale of a call and a put, such as sale of Cisco Mar 20 calls and Mar 20 puts.

strap The purchase of two call options and one put option on the same stock with the same strike price and expiration date, a bullish investment. *See also* strip.

street name The registration of a customer's securities in the name of the brokerage firm, where it is held in the customer's name on the books. Securities held in street name appear on the client's account statement, and dividend and interest payments are deposited into the client's brokerage account.

"the street" A nickname for Wall Street often used to refer to the investment community as a whole.

strike price (*also called the* exercise price) The price at which the owner of an option contract will be entitled to buy the underlying security and the price at which the seller of the contract must deliver the security. In the case of a Microsoft April $27.50 call, $27.50 is the strike price.

strip The purchase of two put options and one call option on the same stock with the same strike price and expiration date, a bearish investment. *See also* strap.

STRIPS An acronym for Separate Trading of Registered Interest and Principal of Securities, securities issued by the U.S. Treasury that are similar to zero-coupon bonds. They are made up of Treasury notes and bonds that have had the interest component "stripped" off, leaving the principal. Interest accrues annually, but is paid at maturity. *See also* zero-coupon bond.

Student Loan Marketing Association (also known as *Sallie Mae*) A publicly owned corporation that buys student loans from the issuing financial institutions and sells them in the secondary market. Sallie Mae guarantees the payment of principal and interest to its investors.

subject quote A tentative quote between broker-dealers in the interdealer market that is subject to confirmation. The market maker may not know the actual bid and ask at the time, or the transaction may be so large the market-maker's firm cannot handle it alone. *See also* firm quote, nominal quote, workout quote.

subordinated debenture A bond that ranks below debentures (unsecured bonds) and secured bonds in claims on assets of a corporation.

subscription right certificate The form through which stockholders who have been given rights exercise the right. The certificate is sent with a check for the purchase price of the new shares to the rights agent to be converted to common stock. *See also* right.

suitability The requirement that any investment made by a broker for a client be consistent with the client's investment objectives, risk tolerance, financial status, age, or income. Unsuitability is one of the problems most often reported to the NASD by investors. An example of unsuitability would be using an elderly client's life savings to buy high-risk options. Clients who suspect unsuitable investments are being bought for them should immediately contact the firm's branch manager or compliance department. *For more information, see* "Common Investor Problems and How to Avoid Them," at www.nasd.com/Investor/Protection/best_practices.asp.

SuperDot (Super Designated Order Turnaround System) A high-speed order entry computer system that routes member firms' market and day limit orders to the proper specialist on the floor of the NYSE. Specialists receiving orders through SuperDot execute them and return reports to the originating firm's offices through the same system. SuperDot can handle daily volume of more than two billion shares.

support The bottom of the trading range within which a stock price fluctuates for a period of time. Technical analysts believe the price of the stock goes down until it meets support, then rises. When stock prices reach their support levels, many stockholders will buy, believing that the stock price will rise. If the price drops below the support level, it is seen as a bearish event. *See also* resistance.

Support

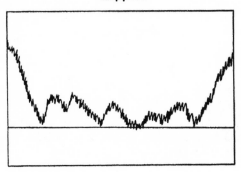

swap *See* bond swap, wash sale.

switch *See* mutual fund switch.

syndicate *See* underwriting syndicate.

syndicate agreement *See* underwriting agreement.

syndicate manager *See* underwriters.

synthetic option The combination of a stock position with options that has the same effect as an option-only position.

Options only	Synthetic Option
Buy call	Buy stock + buy put
Sell call	Sell stock short + sell put
Buy put	Sell stock short + buy call
Sell put	Buy stock + sell call

synthetic stock The equivalent of owning or shorting a stock by buying a call and selling a put on the long side; buying a put and selling a call on the short side.

Stock only	Synthetic Stock
Buy stock	Buy call + sell put
Sell stock short	Buy put + sell call

systematic risk The tendency for prices to move together. In bull markets, stock prices tend to move upward, in bear markets, downward. Stocks within a particular sector or industry, such as airlines or telecommunications companies, often move up and down in price together. *See also* nonsystematic risk.

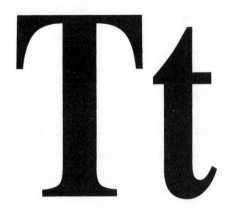

takedown *See* underwriting spread.

takeover arbitrage *See* risk arbitrage.

TAN *See* tax anticipation note.

tape *See* Consolidated Tape.

tax anticipation note (TAN) Short-term securities issued by municipalities, usually when a municipality needs cash temporarily just before a tax collection date. Proceeds from the tax receipts repay the TAN holders. TANs are considered money market securities.

tax-equivalent yield The calculation used to compare taxable securities with those that are tax-exempt. *Example:* Investor L is deciding whether to buy a four percent tax-free bond or a 4.5 percent taxable corporate bond. If the investor's tax rate is 15 percent, the calculation of tax-equivalent yield is as follows:

$$\frac{\text{Tax-free yield}}{100\% - \text{Investor's tax bracket}} = \text{Tax-equivalent yield}$$

$$\frac{4\%}{85\%} = 4.705\%$$

In this case, the tax-equivalent yield on the four percent tax-exempt bond is 4.705 percent, which is higher than the interest on the taxable bond.

T-bill *See* Treasury bill.

T-bond *See* Treasury bond.

technical analysis The use of charts and graphs to study short-term market trends, prices, market activity, and strengths and weaknesses. Technical analysts are more interested in the market as a whole than in the performance of individual companies. Many market analysts use both fundamental and technical analysis for their recommendations–fundamental analysis to choose which stock to buy and technical analysis for timing trades. *For more information*: www.stockcharts.com. *See also* breadth-of-market theory, fundamental analysis, moving average, odd-lot theory, resistance, short-interest theory, support, trend-line, volume-of-trading theory.

tenants in common *See* joint tenants in common (JTIC).

tender option bond *See* put bond.

tender The act of submitting shares of stock or bonds to an issuer in response to an offer to buy back the security.

tender offer An offer to investors to buy stock or bonds, callable or noncallable. The issuer may offer par plus a premium as incentive for investors to tender their bonds. A corporation may extend a tender offer to take back its stock to be held as treasury stock; in an unfriendly takeover move, a competitor may offer a premium as incentive for shareholders to tender their stock.

term bond A debt instrument that is part of a group of bonds that will all mature on the same date. *See also* serial bond.

term maturity The time schedule for maturity of bonds, when the entire issue is redeemed on the same date. *See also* balloon maturity, serial maturity.

third market The over-the-counter market in which institutional investors buy and sell large blocks of exchange-listed stocks.

third-party account A prohibited type of account. An account may not be opened for someone else unless it is an account where a minor is the beneficial owner. An adult may not open an account for another adult, nor trade in the account of someone else, including a spouse, without a power of attorney.

TIGR An acronym for Treasury Investors Growth Receipt, a U.S. government bond that has been stripped of its interest coupons. The remaining principal is sold at a deep discount from face value. Investors do not receive principal payments over the life of the bond but accrued interest is taxable each year. For this reason, most investors hold TIGRs in an IRA or other qualified plan where they grow tax-free. Investors receive full face value at maturity.

time deposit Funds left with commercial or savings banks that the customer has agreed not to withdraw for a specific amount of time. *See also* demand deposit.

time spread *See* calendar spread.

time value The worth of an option beyond its intrinsic value. Options have expiration dates. An option may be out of the money or at the money, with no intrinsic value, three months before its expiration date, but if the market price of the underlying security changes, the option could be in the money before it expires. The longer the time to expiration, the more time value an option has. Time value is reflected in the premium. *Example:* Investor D owns an Oracle March 12.50 call. On December 20 Oracle is selling at $12.50, so the option is at the money and has no intrinsic value. On December 20 the premium for the call is $1.15, so the time value of the call is $1.15 per share.

timing risk The risk that an investor will buy or sell an investment at the wrong time. An investment in the most profitable company may not pay its full profit potential if the investment was timed wrong. *See also* risk.

T-note *See* Treasury note.

TOD account *See* transfer on death account.

tombstone A brief statement of the offering that is the only advertising of a new issue the SEC permits between the filing of a registration statement and SEC approval. Tombstones are restricted to basic information about the offering: name of the issuer, description of the offering, and a list of members of the underwriting group. It must also contain a number of disclaimers: the advertisement does not represent an offer to sell the securities; a registration statement has been filed but is not yet effective; the securities are sold by prospectus only; and a response to the advertisement does not obligate the investor to purchase the security. Tombstones are common in financial newspapers like *The Wall Street Journal.*

trade confirmation *See* confirmation.

trade date The day on which a purchase or sale takes place. *See also* settlement date.

trading authorization Permission given by an account owner to an appointee to make investment decisions for the account. There are two types of trading authorizations, full and limited. A full authorization allows the appointee to deposit or withdraw cash or securities as well as make investment decisions; with a limited trading authorization the appointee may only make investment decisions. *See also* discretionary account.

trading halt A temporary stop to trading in a particular security due to a pending news announcement or to stabilize an imbalance of buy and sell orders. Trading may be halted only at one exchange or it may be suspended in all markets, including over the counter. Since 1989 the exchanges have used collars and circuit breakers to allow stabilization of markets during volatile times. *See* circuit breaker, collar.

tranche A pool of multi-class securities, such as CMOs and REMICs, of one maturity class. *Example:* Tranche A consists of securities with a short maturity, tranche B has medium maturity, and tranche C has longer maturity. Principal payments to a CMO are put into a sinking fund as they are received. When the balance in the sinking fund reaches a certain amount, tranche A is paid off. As more principal is received, the process is repeated until the next tranche is paid off. CMO bonds in the last tranche, Z, are called Z bonds, which are zero-coupon

CMOs. Z bond holders receive no interest payments until tranches A, B, and C are paid off. Z bond holders then receive the remaining cash flow.

transfer agent   An agent, usually a bank or trust company appointed by an issuer, to keep records of stockholders' names, addresses, and social security numbers; receive and cancel sold certificates; issue and deliver stock and bond certificates to shareholders; replace lost, stolen or destroyed certificates; and pay out stock dividends and splits. The transfer agent notifies the registrar of changes of ownership of stocks and bonds. The transfer agent has the final word on whether stock certificates are in good delivery.

transfer on death (TOD) account A brokerage account for which the customer can designate an individual or entity as the beneficiary/owner of the account on the death of the customer. Ownership of the account passes to the beneficiary outside of probate. TOD accounts cover only the cash and securities in the designated account, not personal assets or securities that may be held in a safe-deposit box. Brokerage firms may charge fees to open the account, change beneficiaries, and transfer the assets to the beneficiary.

Treasury bill Short-term investments of one year or less issued by the U.S. Department of the Treasury; they have 4-, 13-, or 26-week maturities, although occasionally some, called cash management bills, have even shorter maturities. T-bills are issued in denominations of $10,000 to $1 million, in $5,000 increments.They are book-entry-only securities. T-bills are quoted at a discount from par because there are no interest payments. For example, a quote of 3.5 percent means that a $10,000 T-bill is selling for 3.5 percent less than face value, or $9,650 ($10,000 x 3.5% = $350, $10,000 - $350 = $9,650). The T-bill matures at its full face value of $10,000.

Treasury bond Long-term investments of 10 to 30 years issued by the U.S. Department of the Treasury in denominations of $1,000 to $1 million; they pay interest every six months. T-bonds and T-notes are priced at a percentage of par in 1/32 increments. For example, a quote of 101:12 means 101 12/32 percent of par, or 101.375. A $10,000 T-bond at that price would cost $10,137.50 ($10,000 x 101.375 percent).

In 2001 the Treasury Department suspended sale of the 30-year bond due to low interest rates. Sales are expected to resume in 2006.

Some Treasury bonds issued before 1985 are callable. The Treasury can call these bonds, many of which are still outstanding, on their first call date, which is five years before maturity, or on any semiannual interest payment date thereafter. The Treasury must give bondholders four months' notice before calling a bond.

Treasury Direct A service of the U. S. Treasury's Bureau of the Public Debt that allows investors to buy Treasury securities directly from the government, without paying brokerage commissions or fees through the website, www.treasurydirect.gov, by phone, or by mail. Treasury Direct holds securities in book-entry form. The minimum investment is $1,000.

Treasury note Intermediate-term investments with maturities of 1 to 10 years issued by the U.S. Department of the Treasury in denominations of $1,000 to $1 million; they pay interest every six months. T-notes and T-bonds are priced at a percentage of par in 1/32 increments. For example, a quote of 101:12 means 101 12/32 percent of par, or 101.375. A $1,000 T-note at that price would cost $1,013.75 ($1,000 x 101.375%).

Treasury receipt Zero-coupon bonds created by brokerage firms with Treasury authorization from U.S. Treasury notes and bonds. Brokers buy Treasury securities and hold them on deposit at a custodian bank. The notes and bonds are separated into principal and interest payments and the receipts are sold separately to investors. *See also* zero-coupon bonds.

treasury stock Stock that a corporation has issued and later repurchased in the secondary market. It is held by the company and can be reissued or retired. Companies may buy back their stock for a number of reasons:.

- If fewer shares are issued, EPS will increase,
- The company can reissue the stock at a later date to generate cash,
- The company can allocate the stock to an employee stock purchase plan or stock options.

Treasury stock is not eligible for dividends and does not carry voting rights. *See also* authorized stock, issued stock, outstanding stock, unissued stock.

trendline The general direction of a stock price; an important tool in technical analysis. Stock prices fluctuate daily, but there is usually a general direction, upward in a bull market or downward in a bear market, that can be charted. *See also* consolidation.

Downtrend	**Uptrend**

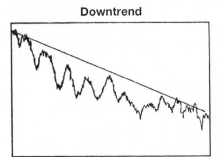 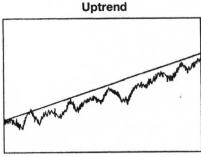

trigger transaction The point where the price of a stock reaches or goes through the price designated on a stop order; at that point, the order changes to a market or limit order. *Example:* A client enters an order to sell 100 XYZ at $50 stop. When the price of XYZ reaches $50, that trigger transaction changes the order to a market order. *See also* stop limit order, stop order.

triple witching day The Friday in March, June, September, and December when stock options, stock index options, and stock index futures all expire. On this day, trading is often volatile as investors try to close contracts before they expire.

trough The bottom of the business cycle, the end of a period of contraction and the beginning of expansion. *See also* business cycle.

trust account A fiduciary arrangement in which the trustee holds legal title to property subject to an obligation to use the property for the benefit of the beneficiary. After a trust is established, usually by a lawyer, assets are placed in the trust. When a trust account is set up, brokerage firms require a copy of the pages of the trust document showing the name and date of the trust and the name of the trustee. If a trustee wants to trade securities on margin, the trust document must specify that margin accounts are allowed.

trustee (1) A person or corporation who manages the investments of a trust on behalf of the trust beneficiary. Trustees must act in accordance with the investment objectives set by the trust. They may not share in any profits in the trust account, but they may charge a reasonable fee for their services. (2) A person or corporation that represents bondholders in dealing with the bond issuer.

trust indenture An agreement between the issuer and a trustee who represents bondholders, containing covenants that outline the issuer's responsibilities toward the bondholders, such as paying all interest and principal; setting rates that will ensure payment of expenses and bond interest; maintaining equipment and property; insuring the property; paying all taxes on the property; ensuring independent audits; and outlining any call features. The federal Trust Indenture Act of 1939 requires that nonexempt corporate bonds be issued with a trust indenture. Though municipal and federal bonds are exempt from the Trust Indenture Act, most municipal revenue bonds are issued with a trust indenture.

Truth in Securities Act *See* Securities Act of 1933.

two-dollar broker (*also called* a competitive trader) A floor broker called in by another floor broker of an exchange who is too busy to handle all the firm's orders. The term comes from the time when the assisting broker was paid two dollars for each round lot trade. Today their commission is negotiable.

type Refers to the two kinds of options, calls and puts. *See also* options.

type 1 account *See* cash account.

type 2 account *See* margin account.

UGMA *See* Uniform Transfer to Minors Act (UTMA).

UIT *See* unit investment trust (UIT).

unauthorized trading Purchase of securities by a broker for a client's account without the client's knowledge or authorization; one of the problems most often reported to the NASD by investors. Clients should always carefully read trade confirmations and account statements. Clients who suspect unauthorized trading should contact the firm's branch manager or compliance department immediately. *For more information:* "Common Investor Problems and How to Avoid Them" at www.nasd.com/Investor/Protection/best_practices.asp.

uncovered option (*also known* as naked position) A position in which an investor in options may be obligated to deliver stock she does not own. An example is uncovered call writing, where the investor accepts the obligation for a set period to sell the underlying security at a predetermined price, at the discretion of the call buyer. If the option is exercised, to sell the stock to the call buyer at the exercise price, the investor will have to buy it at its current price in the open market. There is no theoretical limit as to how high the price might go.

underlying security The primary element of investments such as rights, warrants, convertible securities, or the investment that is bought or sold when an option is exercised. For example, if a GE June 30 call is exercised, the underlying security is General Electric Company common stock. *See also* derivative.

underwriter Investment banking firm that purchases new issues of securities with the intent to distribute them to the public. Often one investment banker, the managing underwriter, negotiates with the issuer to determine the type and size of offering, helps to file the necessary documentation with the SEC, holds due diligence meetings, then invites other investment bankers to form an underwriting syndicate for the purpose of selling the securities. Underwriters are paid fees to promote and sell the securities to the public.

underwriting Acceptance by an investment banker of responsibility for bringing a new security issue to market. The issuer decides how much money it needs from the offering. The underwriter determines if the offering should be stock or bonds and the quantity and price that will yield the required cash for the issuer. The managing underwriter then buys the issue from the company, which provides the capital it needs, less fees (the underwriting proceeds), and the underwriter sells the issue to investors at the public offering price.

Example: A company needs about $1 million to finance its expansion. The managing underwriter arranges for an offering of 100,000 shares of common stock at $10 per share, which brings in gross proceeds of $1,000,000. Of that, $950,000 goes to the issuer. The difference of $50,000, the underwriting spread, pays the managing underwriter and other syndicate members, if there are any.

underwriting agreement An agreement among members of an underwriting syndicate that outlines the responsibilities of and payment arrangements for each member of the syndicate. The most common types of underwriting agreements are (1) firm commitment, (2) best effort, (3) all-or-none, and (4) mini-max. *See also* firm commitment, best effort, all-or-none offering, mini-max offering.

underwriting fee *See* underwriting spread.

underwriting spread The compensation of a syndicate for bringing a new issue to market, generally the difference between the underwriting proceeds and the public offering price. Compensation may consist of:

- Management fee for the managing underwriter.
- Underwriting fee for each member of the syndicate in proportion to the degree of participation of each in bringing the new issue to market. For example, an investment banker responsible for placing 15 percent of the new issue would receive 15 percent of the underwriting fee.
- Concession (also called *reallowance*) allowing members to buy the new security from the syndicate at a discount, "at the concession". For example, selling group members may purchase a new bond issue for a concession of $10, or $990 per bond. The bond's price to the public will be $1,000.
- Takedown, which is similar to a discount. Syndicate members buy the new issue at the "total takedown," which is the price after management and underwriting fees have been deducted. For example, for a $1,000 bond with $975 of the proceeds going to the issuer, a management fee of $4, and an underwriting fee of $5, the total takedown, the price paid by the syndicate members, is $984 ($975 + 4 + 5 = $984). A broker-dealer who is not part of the syndicate would buy the bond at the concession, or $990.

underwriting syndicate Banking firms invited by the underwriting manager to help distribute large stock or bond offerings.

undivided account. *See* Eastern account.

unearned income Income from sources other than wages, salary, commissions, or tips. Examples are dividends, interest, and capital gains from investments. Deductible contributions to individual IRAs cannot be based on unearned income. For example, an investor whose sole income for the year is dividends and capital gains cannot make a tax-deductible contribution to an IRA. *See also* earned income.

unissued stock Stock of a corporation that has been authorized by the state of incorporation but has never been sold or distributed to shareholders. *See also* authorized stock, issued stock, outstanding stock, treasury stock.

Uniform Gifts to Minors Act (UGMA) *See* Uniform Transfer to Minors Act (UTMA).

Uniform Practice Code *See* NASD Manual.

Uniform Securities Act Legislation drafted by the National Conference of Commissioners on Uniform State Laws (NCCUSL) for possible adoption in all the states. The NCCUSL is made up of judges, attorneys, legislators, and law professors from all 50 states who draft proposals for uniform laws to be adopted by the states. *See also* blue-sky laws.

Uniform Transfer to Minors Act (UTMA) A federal law that allows children to own securities, similar to the Uniform Gifts to Minors Act (UGMA). Each state has adopted one or the other law. Each state has established an age of majority, usually between 18 and 21. Children under the age of majority can own securities, but they must be held in UGMA or UTMA accounts, also called custodial accounts. Many types of securities, such as stocks, bonds, insurance, annuities or mutual funds, may be held in custodial accounts. Because the prudent man rule applies to custodial accounts, trading on margin, options, and other risky investments are not permitted. Custodial accounts must contain the name of the custodian and the minor. The tax identification number on the account is the child's social security number. The title on a custodial account is similar to the following, depending on the state in which the account is opened:

(Name of Custodian) as Custodian for
(Name of Minor) a Minor
(Name of State) Uniform (Gift or Transfer) to Minors Act

To open a custodial account, an adult (the donor) deposits cash or securities into the account. There is no maximum contribution amount. The gift is irrevocable. The donor designates a custodian, who may be the donor or another adult. Unlike other fiduciary accounts, no legal documentation naming a custodian is required. The custodian may buy or sell securities and exercise rights or warrants. The custodian controls the account until the child reaches the age of majority, at which time the child takes control of the account. Many brokerage firms will open a new account in the name of the beneficiary at that time. *See also* kiddie tax.

unit A combination of more than one class of security of the same corporation that trades as a single security, such as one share of common stock plus one warrant. Units can be bought and sold just like common stock, the abbreviation "un" follows the name of the stock in newspaper quotes. Units can also be split into their components if an investor wants to keep the common stock and exercise or sell the warrants. *See also* warrant.

unit investment trust (UIT) A type of investment company that is established by a trust indenture. Each UIT has a fixed portfolio of five to 20 securities–stocks, bonds, or both–that are held during the life of the trust. UITs usually begin trading with a one-time public offering of a specific number of units, each representing an undivided interest in the trust. Owners may sell their units at NAV back to the trust or to a trust sponsor (usually a bank or trust company) that maintains a secondary market. Because a UIT has no board of directors or investment manager, proceeds of any securities held in the trust that mature or are redeemed or sold must be paid out to unit owners. A unit trust has a preset termination date on which any securities held will be liquidated and the proceeds distributed to the unit holders. *See also* exchange-traded fund (ETF), investment company.

unit of beneficial interest *See* beneficial interest.

unqualified legal opinion A legal opinion of bond counsel pertaining to the tax-exempt status of a bond that is given without restriction. *See also* qualified legal opinion.

unsolicited order An order that comes voluntarily from the customer. Order tickets to buy or sell securities include a place to mark the trade as solicited or unsolicited. Regulatory agencies and brokerage firms are paying more attention to the solicited/unsolicited status of orders because some brokers were mismarking order tickets as unsolicited when in fact the trades were solicited.

unsuitability *See* suitability.

uptick downtick rule *See* collar.

uptick rule *See* plus tick.

upward trendline *See* trendline.

UTMA *See* Uniform Transfer to Minors Act (UTMA).

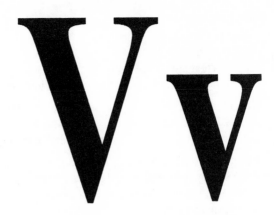

Value Line A source of independent research information for investors. The *Value Line Investment Survey* ranks approximately 1,700 stocks for timeliness and safety. In addition, www.valueline.com has an excellent tutorial for investors.

vertical spread *See* price spread.

vesting The point at which an employee becomes eligible to receive employer contributions to a retirement plan without penalty. The Tax Reform Act of 1986 requires that employers choose either (1) a five-year vesting plan, or (2) 20 percent after three years of service and 100 percent after seven years. When an employee reaches five years of continuous service, 100 percent of all benefits will be non-forfeitable.

visible supply A weekly list of municipal bond issues that are expected to come to the market within the next 30 days, published in *The Bond Buyer.*

volume The number of shares, contracts, or units that trade in a given period. Most stock volume is measured on a daily basis.

volume-of-trading theory The theory that the number of shares trading can give insight into the direction of the market. Technical analysts look at what is happening in large segments of the market, such as the Dow Jones Industrial Average or S&P 500, to find trends in volume and price changes. According to this theory,
- Increasing prices with high volume is bullish.
- Declining prices with low volume is bullish.
- Increasing prices with low volume is bearish.
- Declining prices with high volume is bearish.

voting rights A feature of common stock that allows holders to vote on certain decisions to be made by the corporation. Stockholders may vote at the shareholders' meeting or by proxy. Each stockholder is allowed one vote for each share of stock owned. Stockholders have the right to vote on the following:
- Who should be on the board of directors

• Stock splits
• Whether to issue senior securities
• Significant changes in the corporation's business.

Stockholders do not vote on the amount or payment date of cash or stock dividends. This decision is made by the board of directors. Most preferred stock does not carry voting rights. *See also* cumulative voting rights, statutory voting rights.

voting trust certificates Documents issued to shareholders in exchange for their stock certificates, usually in cases where a company is undergoing financial difficulty and reorganization. A board of trustees, called the voting trust, takes over management of the company and retains voting rights while the trust is in existence. Voting trust certificates give shareholders all rights of ownership except voting. They are transferable, and they are traded like common stock. At the termination of the voting trust, new stock certificates are issued to shareholders in exchange for their voting trust certificates.

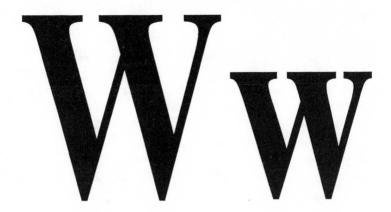

Wall Street The location of the NYSE in New York City. The term is also used to mean the investment community in general.

warrant A right to buy a stock at a specified price before a preset date. Warrants are often issued as part of a bond offering; they last longer than rights. The exercise price of a warrant at the time of issue is higher than the market price of the underlying stock. Warrants trade just like stock; the symbol "wt" follows the name of the stock. Warrants can be exercised at any time before they expire. They have ex-warrant dates; as with dividends, the ex-warrant date is two business days before record date. *See also* ex-dividend date.

wash sale The process of selling and then buying the same security, or put or call options on the same security, within 30 days before or 30 days after the date of sale (61 days). The IRS prohibits an investor from deducting any loss on such an investment. For example, if an investor sells for a loss on May 12, the loss may not be deducted if replacement stock is purchased between April 12 and June 11.

30 days before	Trade Date	30 days after
April 12	May 12	June 11

The end of the tax year does not affect the wash sale rule. If an investor sells at a loss and her husband buys the stock within the 61-day period, it is also considered a wash sale. *See also* bond swap.

Western account (*also known as* divided account) A method of underwriting securities issues in which members of the underwriting syndicate act severally but not jointly and thus do not share the risk of unsold shares. If some firms cannot sell their shares, the cost of those shares is borne only by those firms. *See also* Eastern account.

when-issued (WI) (*also known as* when-, as- and if-issued) Confirmation of the purchase of securities, such as municipal bonds and corporate spin-offs, that can be bought and sold before their issue date, which is the date when the certificates are issued. A when-issued confirmation contains the quantity, description, and price of the security, and whether the broker acted as dealer, but no dollar or settlement date information. The description carries a WI notation. When the security is ready to begin trading, the investor will receive a new confirmation with the amount due and the settlement date on it.

Investors who wish to sell securities before they are distributed may deliver a due bill to the buyer that promises to deliver the stock once it is issued or they may sell on a when-issued basis. The NASD Uniform Practices Committee determines the settlement date for when-issued securities. See also confirmation.

WI *See* when-issued.

Wilshire 5000 Index *(also called the* Dow Jones Wilshire 5000 index) The world's largest index by market value. The Wilshire 5000 is a weighted index of all U.S.-headquartered equity securities with readily-available price data. The index follows more than 5,000 stocks and is the best measure of the entire U.S. stock market.

withholding *See* backup withholding.

workable indication The bid price at which one dealer is willing to buy a security from another. The first dealer is allowed to change its bid if market conditions change.

working capital A synonym for liquidity, the amount of money a company has available to meet short-term obligations. The formula for working capital is:

Working capital = Current assets - Current liabilities

workout quote Quote of an approximate price rather than a firm quote given by one broker-dealer to another when the market maker knows the order will require special handling. *For example*, a broker may have a large order that will cause disruption to the market or a normal order in a thin or unstable market. *See also* firm quote, nominal quote, subject quote.

writer The seller of an option contract. *See also* call writer, put writer.

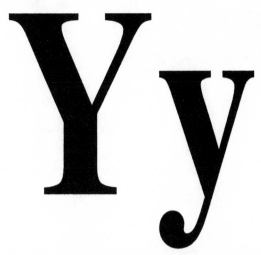

Yellow Sheets A daily quotation service for corporate bonds traded over the counter. It lists recent bid and ask prices for each brokerage firm that makes a market in the bonds. The name comes from the color of the paper they are printed on. *See also* Pink Sheets.

yield The rate of return; how much an investor can expect to earn on an investment. It is usually expressed as a percentage. There are a number of ways to express yield. *See also* coupon yield, current yield, dividend yield, nominal yield, tax-equivalent yield, yield to call, yield to maturity.

yield curve A graph showing the relationship between interest rates and time. The horizontal axis represents time, the vertical axis interest rates.

If short-term interest rates are lower than long-term rates, the yield curve is called *normal or positive*; this is the most common pattern.

Positive Yield Curve

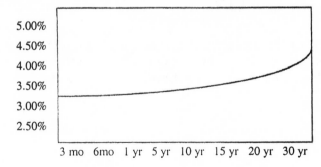

If short-term interest rates are higher than long-term rates, the yield curve is called *inverted or negative.*

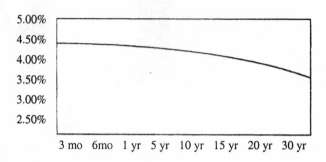

Negative Yield Curve

If there is little difference between short-term and long-term interest rates, the yield curve is called *flat.*

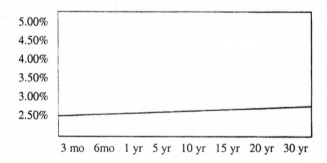

Flat Yield Curve

yield to call (YTC) The rate of return an investor would receive on a bond if it were called on its first call date. Bonds issued with a call date must be quoted with the yield to call instead of yield to maturity.

yield to maturity (YTM) The rate of return an investor would receive on a bond if it were held until maturity. It is the same as the coupon yield only if the bond is purchased at par. The steps to calculate yield to maturity are:

$$\text{Annual interest} \frac{+ \text{ Discount, or}}{- \text{ Premium}} = \text{Annual return on investment (ROI)}$$

$$\frac{\text{Purchase price} + \text{Par value}}{2} = \text{Average price}$$

$$\frac{\text{Annual return on investment (ROI)}}{\text{Average price}} = \text{Yield to maturity}$$

Example: A $1,000 5% bond is bought at a premium of 102 ($1,020):

1. Annual interest ($1,000 x 5% = $50) minus premium ($1,020 - $1,000 = $20) = annual return on investment ($30).
2. Purchase price ($1,020) plus par value ($1,000) divided by 2 = average price ($1,010).
3. Annual return on investment ($30) divided by average price ($1,010) = .0297 = 2.97% YTM.

YTM on a $1,000 5% bond bought at a discount of 98 ($980) would be:

1. Annual interest ($1,000 x 5% = $50) plus discount ($1,000 - $980 = $20) = annual return on investment ($70).
2. Purchase price ($980) plus par value ($1,000) divided by 2 = average price ($990).
3. Annual return on investment ($70) divided by average price ($990) = .0707 = 7.07% YTM.

YTC *See* yield to call.

YTM *See* yield to maturity.

Z bond A zero-coupon CMO. Z bonds are the final tranche of a class of maturities to receive principal and interest payments. Z bond holders receive no interest payments until tranches A (short-term maturity), B (medium-term maturity), and C (long-term maturity) are paid off. Z bond holders then receive the remaining cash flow. *See also* tranche.

zero-coupon bond Bonds created by brokerage firms using U. S. Treasury notes and bonds. The brokers detach the coupon (interest) payments from the principal and sell them separately. Zero-coupon bonds are the repackaged principal of the underlying bonds. They do not pay interest; instead, they are sold at a deep discount. *For example*, a $1,000 face value zero-coupon bond that yields three percent and matures in 20 years would cost about $550. At maturity, the investor would receive $1,000.

Zero-coupon bonds have several advantages. Since there are no interest payments, there is no reinvestment risk. They are also extremely liquid, having an active secondary market. Investors have the benefit of choosing a maturity date and knowing exactly how much the investment will be worth at maturity.

Among their disadvantages is that they are more sensitive to interest rates than equivalent bonds with interest payments. Also, if held in a taxable account, zero-coupon bonds are taxed as if they pay annual interest. The accretion of the bond discount, the increase in value each year, is taxable.

Some brokerage firms give interesting acronyms to the zero-coupon bonds they issue, such as CATS (Certificates of Accrual on Treasury Securities), TIGRs (Treasury Investment Growth Receipts), and COUGRs (Certificates of Government Receipts).

zero minus tick A last trade that is at the same price as the trade immediately before it but lower than the one before that. For example, if a stock trades at 25, then 24.80, it is a minus tick. If the next trade is again 24.80, it is a zero minus tick. *See also* minus tick.

zero plus tick A last trade that is at the same price as the trade immediately before it but higher than the one before that. For example, if a stock trades at 45, then 45.125, it is a plus tick. If the next trade is again 45.125, it is a zero plus tick. Orders to sell short may be executed only on a plus tick or zero plus tick. *See also* plus tick, short sale.

Acronyms

The following acronyms are used throughout:

ACATS	Automated Customer Account Transfer Service System
ADR	American depository receipt
AGI	Adjusted gross income
AMEX	American Stock Exchange
BSE	Boston Stock Exchange
CBOE	Chicago Board Options Exchange
CBOT	Chicago Board of Trade
CFTC	Commodity Futures Trading Corporation
CHX	Chicago Stock Exchange
CMO	Collateralized mortgage obligation
CSE	Cincinnati Stock Exchange
DJIA	Dow Jones Industrial Average
ECN	Electronic communications network
EPS	Earnings per share
ERISA	Employee Retirement Income Security Act
ETF	Exchange-traded fund
FDIC	Federal Deposit Insurance Corporation
FHA	Federal Housing Authority
FNMA	Federal National Mortgage Association
GNMA	Government National Mortgage Association
GDP	Gross domestic product

IPO	Initial public offering
IRA	Individual retirement account
IRS	Internal Revenue Service
Merc	Chicago Mercantile Exchange
NASD	National Association of Securities Dealers
NAV	net asset value
NYSE	New York Stock Exchange
OCC	Office of Controller of the Currency
OTC	Over the counter
PCX	Pacific Stock Exchange
PHLX	Philadelphia Stock Exchange
POP	Public offering price
Reg T	Regulation T of the Securities Exchange Act of 1934
SEC	Securities and Exchange Commission
SIPC	Securities Investor Protection Corporation
SRO	Self-regulatory organization
UGMA	Uniform Gifts to Minors Act
UIT	Unit investment trust
UTMA	Uniform Transfers to Minors Act
VA	Veterans Administration

Websites

www.cboe.com/LearnCenter/pdf/DJX-DIAbrochure.pdf - Index options info

www.collegesavings.org

www.djindexes.com

www.dowjones.com

www.FederalReserveEducation.org

www.nasd.com

www.nyse.com

www.russell.com/US/Indexes

www.savingforcollege.com

www.sec.com

www.sec.gov/edgar/searchedgar/webusers.htm - search the EDGAR database

www.sec.gov/investor/pubs/margin.htm - borrowing to buy stocks on margin

www.sipc.org

www.smartmoney.com - Map of the Market - S&P 500

www.standardandpoors.com

www.stockcharts.com - technical analysis using charts

www.valueline.com

About TEXERE

Texere, a progressive and authoritative voice in business publishing, brings to the global business community the expertise and insights of leading thinkers. Our books educate, enlighten, and entertain, and provide an intersection where our authors and our readers share cutting edge ideas, practices, and innovative solutions. Texere seeks to cultivate, enhance, and disseminate information that illuminates the global business landscape.

www.thomson.com/learning/texere

About the typeface

This book was set in 10 point Times Roman. In 1931, The Times of London commissioned a new type design for the body copy of the paper. The design process was supervised by Stanley Morison. Times is actually a modernised version of the older typeface "Plantin", which Morison was instructed to use as the main basis for his new designs. Times font became the workhorse of the publishing industry and continues to be very popular, particularly for newspapers, magazines, and corporate communications such as proposals and annual reports. Due to its versatility, it remains a must-have typeface for today's designer.

Library of Congress Cataloging-in-Publication Data

Martz, Catharyn.
    Dictionary of investment terms / Catharyn Martz.
        p. cm.
    ISBN 0-324-20352-7 (hardcover : alk. paper)
    1. Investments--Dictionaries. I. Title.
    HG4513.M37 2006
    332'.03--dc22

                                        2005027386